PSYCHOLOGY RESEARCH PROGRESS

THE OTHER SIDE OF THE COIN

THE PSYCHOLOGICAL IMPLICATIONS OF MICROCREDIT

PSYCHOLOGY RESEARCH PROGRESS

Additional books in this series can be found on Nova's website under the Series tab.

Additional e-books in this series can be found on Nova's website under the e-book tab.

ECONOMIC ISSUES, PROBLEMS AND PERSPECTIVES

Additional books in this series can be found on Nova's website under the Series tab.

Additional e-books in this series can be found on Nova's website under the e-book tab.

PSYCHOLOGY RESEARCH PROGRESS

THE OTHER SIDE OF THE COIN

THE PSYCHOLOGICAL IMPLICATIONS OF MICROCREDIT

LUISA BRUNORI
AND
MALCOLM PINES
EDITORS

nova publishers
New York

For permission to use material from this book please contact us:
Telephone 631-231-7269; Fax 631-231-8175
Web Site: http://www.novapublishers.com

Library of Congress Cataloging-in-Publication Data

The other side of the coin : the psychological implications of microcredit / editors, Luisa Brunori and Malcolm Pines (Department of Psychology, University of Bologna, Bologna, Italy).
pages cm
Includes bibliographical references and index.
ISBN 978-1-62618-726-9 (hardcover)
1. Microfinance. 2. Finance--Psychological aspects. I. Brunori, Luisa.
HG178.3.O84 2013
332--dc23

2013013151

Published by Nova Science Publishers, Inc. † New York

CONTENTS

FOREWORD

I am very delighted to hear that my friend Professor Luisa Brunori of University of Bologna, Italy and her colleague, Dr. Malcolm Pines from England, who is known all over the world for his work in the field of Group Analysis, have come together to edit a book on microcredit. Microcredit has already been researched from different theoretical and practical perspectives. Professor Brunori is one of the few group psychologists who understands the importance of viewing microcredit through an analytical point of view and I find myself to be in agreement with her regarding the fact that more research should be done from this perspective.

In Grameen, the ideas of trust, group unity and relationships have been the chief influences towards its success and I feel that it is these ideas that are also found in Professor Brunori's work in-group analysis. We place trust in people, and in turn, they trust us. "Credit" means "trust". Over the years we have been able to transform this trust into hope in the group. This group membership creates group support and group pressure, which smoothens out behavioral patterns and makes borrowers more reliable. A sense of inter-group and intra-group competition helps everyone try to be an achiever. Over time this practice of group leadership also gave birth to community leadership in the society, which is a great achievement of the trust based Grameen credit mechanism.

This book emphasizes these issues along with the psychosocial and economic aspects of microcredit through Grameen Bank and other experiences. The authors explore several aspects of microcredit which include the understanding of the needs, desires and potentialities between nature and culture, whether human beings are naturally or culturally self-interested and whether it is possible for human beings to produce the best for the development of their potentialities for themselves as human beings and for the community and the society.

People are not one-dimensional entities but are rather very multi-dimensional. Their emotions, beliefs, priorities, and behavior can best be compared to the millions of shades we can create from the three primary colors. Through trust, support and solidarity, many resources can be developed for the benefit of Individuals, community and society.

The unique characteristics of this book can be best described as the intertwining between tangible and intangible aspects of the productive process of microcredit and the psychological aspect of microcredit experiences and their consequences.

Professor Muhammad Yunus
Dhaka, January 2013

PREFACE

Everything started in the year 2000 when, in the frame of the *Group Analytic Society, London* (G.A.S.) event, a Winter Workshop was decided to be held in Venice. The title was *Money and its meaning, starting from the group* and had been decided according to several discussions on the economical consistency of our Association. Besides that, the process of the passage from European coins into Euro was going on at that time.

The event was very successful and opened a wide area of thinking on a subject, economy, that appeared to be much less *"concrete"* and much more "*relational*" than we could ever imagined.

"Relational goods" had become a key word and were considered to be included in a frame that could develop a common understanding of both tangible and intangible aspects of relations and of human resources.

Precursor had been a conference in Bologna University in 1999 that had brought the attention to a research in the field of the Managed Care System in the Welfare State. Costs and benefits in clinical psychological applications; *groups versus individual settings* have been a further step leading to a concept: *The economy of the group in the managed care system. Between Psychopharmacological interventions and interminable analysis* that was the starting point of this important process of knowledge.

The conference on *The Economy of the group: the emergence of Relational goods in Society, mind and brain* in 2002 at Bologna University again with the Group Analytic Society has been the third step of the development of this area of research.

Again a big success and a lot of interest was developed about a subject that seemed to announce a wide area of new knowledge inside a fruitful exchange between Economics and Group Analysis.

Group analytic thinking appeared to be the more comprehensive psychodynamic frame of reference to contain such a discussion, because of the wide area of intertwining concepts crossing social sciences where economics, in its etymological sense of *the rule of the family home* (*oikòs nomos*) could be seen and understood.

Besides that, Polanyi contribution in the frame of Frankfurt School in which Group Analysis was rooted and generated was a further inspiration in his expression *"economics embedded in Society"* meaning, by that, the importance of mind creation in the development of economical thinking and action for both Individuals and Society.

It was in this frame of exchange that Malcolm Pines told me "do you know, Luisa, that in Bangladesh there is an incredible man, an economist that gives loans to groups of women on trust?!"

I had the fortunate opportunity to meet Muhammad Yunus in Bologna few months later and literally fall in love with his fantastic ideas that never occurred to me to think so clearly but that were already under trace in my mind and in the works that we were running in those times!

Christmas holidays in Bangladesh in 2002, allowed me to see by my own eyes and understand directly.

It has been a real fantastic discovery, something that opened my heart and my mind to a new fantastic adventure that still is producing in me a great enthusiastic sense that something can be done for human beings.

Since then a fantastic research group has been created together with several interesting initiatives that have been able to generate this book that represents, at this stage, the result of a wonderful journey with colleagues that have become friends of a dream that has proved to be possible where psychology can contribute to generate a *"relational land"* where people can create what they need to live dignified lives.

This work could have never been possible without alliance and common effort with Malcolm Pines.

I want to thank Malcolm for that.

Luisa Brunori

INTRODUCTION

In the last UN meetings looking at the Millennium Development Goals, poverty has been seen as one of the main reasons for social violence at all levels both locally and internationally or a fuel for that.

Besides the ethical point of view that should include human rights policy, the economical view should also be taken into account from a Human Development Index (HDI) perspective, instead of the Gross Domestic Product (GDP) approach.

The present economic situation and, in particular, some of its international dynamics, including the globalization process, appear to be leading to conflict and war. The "*Homo Oeconomicus*" is philosophically, a human being organized in a way that leads to a conflict resolution, in which war is seen as the "obvious" consequence, in spite of the conceptual declarations of a generalized will of peace.

This statement is commonly recognized as such and corresponds to an accredited position in the criticism to the dominant economical thinking actually named as "main stream".

On the other hand, different socio-economical experiences have been developed according to parameters that take into special account the needs of individuals seen as human beings: the Human Development Index mentioned previously is one of them.

In this frame of thinking, poverty is seen as an aberration of socio-economical development. If the latter ideally leads to global wide positive change (or at least there is a declaration of intention towards this aim), sometimes the outcome is increasing disparity between countries and people to such an extent that it produces a series of discontent and aggressiveness, difficult to manage in a globally expanded civil society.

Such a process, in fact, in spite of the declared intentions, tends to create a social pathology, which, in turn, generates losses of various kinds, both tangible and intangible in people's lives.

Microcredit is one of those virtuous experiences accredited as a very special and effective tool for fighting against poverty and injustice, valuing social trust and individual creativity, through a circle between individual development and that of the Community.

In fact, through the development of a social-individual relationship, based on a win-win philosophy, the possibility to create richness is realized to a great extent.

Normally, studies about social and economical intertwining tend to refer to human beings as part of categories socially determined according to a view of a Society organized in social groups.

Actually, with the help of new technologies, a new mental representation of Society is possible and can be effectively created.

The "World Wide Web" allows people to have a vision of a Society composed of individuals connected through nets. Studies on Complexity and social relations offer the possibility to understand a social dynamism that, starting from the individual, can reach the "www" dimension through a series of different aspects of the self, seen in a continuous creation of subjective identities.

Microcredit represents a realization connected to this vision of the world and of the social structure in which the interaction between the Individual and the Society through (and involving) the Community in which people live is in favor of both: the Society and Individuals.

The experience started in Bangladesh is one of the most inspiring social innovations of the last decades based on this win-win philosophy and on the benefits that both entities can get through their virtuous interaction.

So inspiring is this experience that his "inventor" has been awarded the 2006 Nobel Peace Prize. "The fact that a Peace Nobel Prize has been assigned to an Economist as I am, means that Peace is recognized as a result of Economical assumptions and practice". With these words Yunus started his Nobel Peace Prize Lecture in December 2006, in Oslo.

From the poorest country, microcredit expanded all over the world and involved more than one hundred million people in all continents.

Many are the experiences of microcredit in the world but what Yunus has done has had such a special value in terms of creating not only economical development but, most importantly, respect and citizenship.

In fact, not only beneficiaries have been given the opportunity to overcome poverty through small loans given on trust to individuals organized in groups with shared responsibility, but each of them has been offered the possibility to become owner of the Bank.

As a consequence of this, the Nobel Prize was jointly awarded to Yunus and to the Grameen bank as an Organization.

The meaning of this choice is clearly oriented towards offering to these people, besides the loan, the rights of human beings, the recognition of their value for their Community and the dignity of citizens able to contribute to the community's needs through their capabilities. "Now, Grameen women stand for elections" says Yunus with pride.

This event took place in a very poor region of the country, Jobra and involved the more depressed part of the population: women. Now more than eight million people own the Grameen Bank and 97% are women.

What is so important in this experience, besides the tangible aspects of it, are the psychological and relational ones for the individuals involved as a consequence of trust. In fact, this offer was able to create in these women such a sense of value, self esteem and pride that their state of tremendous poverty could turn into a state of hope and possibility to run a so called "normal life": "like the others".

Richness, in fact has not only been seen through its tangible and concrete results but also in terms of social inclusion and participation in the Community.

From one side, this process has been able to develop individual resources making richness out of the capabilities of those people whose contribution had never been valued and, vice-versa, it has created the possibility for the same people to understand how to relate to community needs.

Microcredit is an *operational and policy instrument* turned into a powerful *interpretative device*. The path-breaking conception of Muhammad Yunus has radically modified standard approaches to economic and social development, primarily by emphasizing the role of trust-enforcing social arrangements, their roots in reciprocal interactions and their influence upon individual trustworthiness. The success of microcredit experiments calls for a rethinking of the theory of social action in connection with economic patterns of interdependence. In particular, microcredit points to the embedding of economic interactions within social and institutional networks, highlights the role of embedding in promoting the functioning of capabilities, and emphasizes that responsible choices pre-suppose an adequate network of mutual influences and constraints. At the same time, microcredit calls attention to freedom of choice and personal initiative in taking full advantage of relational structures, achieving a satisfactory functioning of human capabilities and realizing trustworthiness through civic and social engagement.

In: The Other Side of the Coin
Editors: L. Brunori and M. Pines

ISBN: 978-1-62618-726-9

Chapter 1

MICROCREDIT EXPERIENCE FROM TANGIBLE AND INTANGIBLE PERSPECTIVES

Luisa Brunori*
Department of Psychology, University of Bologna

ABSTRACT

This chapter aims to give an overview of what Microcredit is, how it works and which are the main characteristics of it. The intertwining between tangible and intangible goods in the Microcredit process is explored, underlining the complexity of this tool.

The chapter starts with a description of what microcredit is, the development of it, and how it was transformed from its first version (Grameen 1) to its second version (Grameen 2).

Then there is an analysis of the inspirational principal (trust, women, the group and its potential, credit, practice, self-employment), and a special focus on the social rules and the XVI decisions of the Grameen bank.

Different aspects of poverty (intra- psychic poverty, shame, social exclusion) are touched, in order to show how microcredit in its complexity can have an impact on those intangible aspects of people's life.

---

* Correspondence regarding this chapter may be addressed to Luisa Brunori, *luisa.brunori@unibo.it*.

INTRODUCTION

What is particularly interesting in Yunus' experience is the intertwining between tangible and intangible goods in a cause/effect process.

In fact, starting from intangible goods: trust, tangible goods (products from the activity) are developed that, in their turn, generate self-esteem, intangible; that again, develops the capability for risk taking behavior that further on develops resources (tangible) and so on, through a virtuous crescendo that takes place inside a relational goods system.

This is the reason why this circularity should be better understood in its dynamics to allow a better knowledge in the frame of psychology and economics towards a possible sustainable dialogue.

Before we start our discussion about Microcredit and its effects on tangible and intangible goods, a little explanation of what Microcredit is and how it developed is necessary.

In fact microcredit consist in an innovative way of money lending that is based upon giving little loans to people excluded from the traditional bank system, allowing them to realize little enterprises or to consolidate already existing activities.

Microcredit is a development tool for the potentials of socially emarginated people on the territory, for the development of autonomy, for a parallel and not passivizing welfare, for the recovery of self esteem, for reformulating internal/external and individual/group dialectic through re-elaboration of the social contents of the relation.

WHAT IS MICROCREDIT?

Microcredit, in its modern definition, started from the ideas of Yunus, a teacher of economics in Bangladesh. Yunus, trying to find a solution to end poverty in his country, Bangladesh, observed that a big constrain poor people face is their exclusion from formal financial services, fundamental in order to create income opportunities. “The poor, who lack collateral, receive nothing from banks because they have nothing to offer. As a result, more than half of the world's population is deprived of the financial services of conventional banks” (Yunus, 2007, p.20).

This formal exclusion from capital was identified as the missing element in the struggle of the poor against poverty, as “the most important step to ending poverty is the creation of employment and income opportunities for the poor" (Yunus, 2007, p.21), and without any access to finance the creation of employment and income opportunities lack of a fundamental mean. The assumption of Yunus was that if individual borrowers are given access to credit, they will be able to identify and engage in viable income-generating activities. In order to overcome the problem of the denied access to finance to the poor, he created a new system of banking, to give access to credit to the poor. "A new system of banking [...] focused not on profit but on the needs of its borrowers. Such banks are built with a different mission in mind: the objective is to bring financial services to the impoverished" (Yunus, 2007, p.20).

Grameen Bank and Microcredit[1]

In 1971 Bangladesh gained its independence after which it fell into a deep crisis. The whole country was struck by great famine between 1974-1975.In 1975 Prof. Yunus became a Professor of Economics of Chittagong University. His house was situated in Chittagong city. To go to University he had to walk through a village named Jobra.

Prof. Yunus' 'first attempt to alleviate hunger involved a program to improve agricultural productivity through irrigation.' Though it was a successful project, he was not satisfied as he realized later that the poor received almost no benefit from it as they did not own the land and most of them were daily laborers. He then tried to understand the deep root cause of people's sufferings and tried to spend as much time as possible with those who lived in Jobra village. One of the most important causes of poverty that he found later on was the money lending nature in the village. Heavy reliance on moneylenders and unimaginable high interest rates made it impossible for local people to move out of poverty. It struck him like nothing else. With one of his students he carried out a research within the village and found out that there were 42 people who had taken out a loan from local moneylenders that amounted to of no less than $27 per person. He then decided to offer the equivalent of this $27 out of his own pocket to get these victims out of the

---

[1] For the writing of this paragraph I made use of the information provided by Shamimur Rahman, currently a research fellow at the International Observatory on Microfinance (MY), University of Bologna, where he conducts research on microcredit after having been a collaborator of the Grameen Bank in Bangladesh.

clutches of the moneylenders. The excitement that was created among the people by this small action got him further involved in it.

Once Prof. Yunus realized that a small lending project would benefit the most disadvantaged people he went to the local bank to ask for funding. The bank rejected the project on the grounds that poor people were not creditworthy. Consequently he decided to act as guarantor and asked the bank to give him the fund. In turn he would then be able to provide poor people with the money they needed. The Bank agreed to this plan and a small microcredit operation started. As the Prof. Yunus had imagined, his small microcredit venture was extremely successful with extremely high repayment rates. However, the professor's mindset of the traditional banker never changed, he kept persisting and in 1977 he was able to convince Bangladesh Bank to open 'a special bank in Jobra to test the idea of lending to the poor.' The name of the project was called the 'experimental Grameen Branch. It enjoyed the same kind of success as the earlier, informal efforts, including nearly perfect repayment rates. Although the program started in Chittagong, the second biggest city in Bangladesh, it was not easy to expand the program in other parts of the country. Prof. Yunus, after much opposition from the government, eventually overcame the issues. He, however, also wanted to create a separate bank for the poor, one that would give loans without the need for collateral, without requiring a credit history and free from constricting regulations. He continued appealing to the government and requests the permission to convert their project into a special bank under a separate law. In 1983, the bank for the poor was born under new laws created especially for the purpose. It was named Grameen Bank.

Why the Transformation from Grameen 1 to Grameen 2 Became Obvious?

Over the years we occasionally tried adding new rules and amending specific features of the basic Grameen system without conducting any major overhaul of the entire program. As a result Grameen system remained a one-size-fit all programs that worked generally well but could not address any special needs that borrowers might have. After fifteen years of operation, Grameen was ripe for change-and the great flood of 1998 provided the opportunity for a major upgrade of the system [Table 1]. A hallmark of Grameen 1 was group fund, the purpose of which was to act as a mini-bank for the group. Five percent of each loan plus a fixed weekly amount was deposited into this fund. The borrowers, with the approval of group members, could borrow from the fund for many reasons, but they had to pay the loan back within agreed-upon time. Before 1995 Grameen borrowers could not access group funds other than for short term withdrawal subject to approval by the group that had to be repaid. Even though borrowing from the group fund was interest free, borrowers had to pay 5% group tax, known as group tax 2 on these loans. More important, borrowers who dropped out could not claim their share of group fund.

Table 1. The difference between Grameen 1 and Grameen 2

Grameen 1	Grameen 2	Reason for change
No provision to save for pension.	Borrower deposits a fixed monthly amount in Grameen pension scheme	To help borrowers build a nest egg retirement
Fixed, one size fits all savings program.	Varied savings plans to fit member's individual needs	To encourage savings for special needs and long term economic benefit.
No initiative to collect savings from members.	Active campaigns to collect savings from non members	To enable the bank to self fund future loans
Mostly one year loans with fixed installment amounts.	Loan duration and installment size	To allow borrowers to tailor loan products to individual needs and changing circumstances
Common loan ceilings for an entire branch.	Individual loan ceilings based on savings and other measurements	To reward and incentivize good borrowing and repayment practices by members.
Family responsible for loan of deceased borrower.	Special savings fund ensures that outstanding loans are paid off after death	To alleviate borrowers fears of leaving debt behind after death
Borrower becomes defaulter if loan is not repaid in 52 weeks.	Borrower becomes defaulter if repayment schedule is not met within six months	To create an early warning signal of potential borrower problems
Funds for new bank branches borrowed from head office at 12 percent interest.	New branches are self funding from day 1, using savings from borrowers and non borrowers.	To ensure that branches become self sufficient quickly.

Grameen bank which attained its formal status in 1983 faced a repayment problem in 1998 in the aftermath of an unprecedented flood that inundated two thirds of Bangladesh for thirteen weeks from June to September. Even though 80% of the borrowers repaid on time, the other 20% lost all contact with the bank. This loss affected the whole system. The rigidity of the rules and the precarious nature of the poor's existence increased the debt burden of the borrowers so much so that they stopped coming to the center meetings to make payments.

In some areas a combination of difficult geography, post flood decline in economic activity, staff neglect, and a breakdown of repayment culture created serious problems for the bank; the members discontinued their installment payments and attendance in the regular weekly meetings, and staff lost contact with members completely. But the flood was only a mere cause for this problem. Together the staff and the management came to the conclusion that the rigid rules of Grameen Bank 1 were the main contributing factor to the problem. The result is Grameen 2.

The repayment problems in the late 90's made Grameen bank the transformation but there were borrower revolution and staff anger even before that. These happened because of the rigid payment system and inability to withdraw savings from the group fund. But each of these happenings made GB management think about an overhaul of the program itself. .

Group Liabilities to Individual Lending

The most important change to the classical Grameen Model is that the group is no longer liable for individual loans, meaning that the group no longer has to provide a guarantee for the loan to its members. This change in level of responsibility from group to individual does not mean that there is no longer a role for groups. In Grameen 1, groups were used to simplify the collection of repayments, to reduce transaction costs of loan collection, and to support members in need. In some Grameen Bank branches the local staff made other borrowers in the group liable for a member's missed payments, but restricted the practice by imposing a limit of a maximum period of four weeks. After twenty five years of observing the negative aspects of groups, however, the bank decided to invert the structure by rewarding an individual borrower for the success of the group as a whole and blending the group responsibility. Previously, if everyone in the group performed well, there was no reward, but if some members performed badly, the group had to deal with the stigma. Now, groups are rewarded for their good performance.

The funding principle of group lending-the use of the group as a point of service-still applies. Center meetings of groups are still being used to build social capital by promoting norms of good behavior, networking to share information about health and business opportunities, and building trust beyond the narrow radius of trust that encompassed only family members.

Members view groups as a reflection of accountability and permanence. The bank strongly believes that the center meeting of groups is an important forum for borrowers that continue to ensure the transparency of financial transactions

A hallmark of Grameen 1 was group fund, the purpose of which was to act as a mini-bank for the group. Five percent of each loan plus a fixed weekly amount was deposited into this fund. The borrowers, with the approval of group members, could borrow from the fund for many reasons, but they had to pay the loan back within agreed-upon time. Before 1995 Grameen borrowers could not access group funds other than for short term withdrawal subject to approval by the group that had to be repaid. Even though borrowing from the group fund was interest free, borrowers had to pay 5% group tax, known as group tax 2 on these loans. More important, borrowers who dropped out could not claim their share of group fund. In Grameen 2 the notion of group fund has been abandoned. Instead, borrowers are offered individual accounts.

The main differences between Grameen 1 and Grameen 2: Instead of several loan products as under Grameen 1, there is now one prime loan product: the basic loan. The duration of the loan can vary from three months to three years, as opposed to the typical one year loan under Grameen1. The installment size can also vary during the loan period and can be tailored to meet the needs of the borrowers. Under Grameen 1, loans were staggered, with two members receiving their loans first, then another two, and then typically the group chairperson. Now all members can receive loans at the same time. More-over, instead, of being disbursed at one time, loan amounts can be disbursed at one time, loan amounts can be disbursed in tranches under Grameen 2. Previously, a borrower could not receive a new loan without fully repaying a loan of same type. Under Grameen 2, with the exception of special investment and housing loans, a member can borrow the amount repaid after six months without having to repay the original loan in full. A borrower can also repay the loan in a large, lump-sum amount, which was not allowed in Grameen 1. A borrower under classical Grameen was branded a defaulter if she could not repay the full amount of a loan within fifty-two weeks. Now she will be labeled a defaulter if she cannot repay the due amount per schedule within six months or twenty six weeks, and instead of defaulting, she has the temporary option of switching to a flexible loan contract. Under Grameen 1, failure to repay the installment was the only way a borrower could become in arrears. Now a borrower can also become a defaulter if she fails to make deposit for four consecutive months in her GPS account.

The method of setting the loan ceilings has also changed under the new model. In Grameen 1, a common loan ceiling existed for all borrowers of a branch. Under Grameen 2, each borrower has her own ceiling, which depends on her performance and the performance of the group, center and branch, as well as the amount of her savings. Under Grameen 1, there was no hard and fast rule about increasing and decreasing the loan ceiling; under Grameen 2, the loan ceiling is affected by the size of savings deposits, frequency of attendance at center meetings, and the overall performance of the borrower, her group, her center, and the branch. Group fund savings have been eliminated under Grameen 2. Another change is in the amount of weekly savings. In Grameen 1 weekly savings were uniform, while under the current regime weekly savings are tied to the loan amounts.

Structure and operation of GB: Different offices, borrowers, groups, loans.

The management structure of the bank is one characteristic that has retained its original form. The lowest administrative unit of the bank is the branch, which typically consists of a branch manager, a senior assistant, several bank workers, and a peon cum guard. A branch usually manages eighty centers, each of which consists of six to eight groups. The bank worker known as the center manager is in charge of ten centers.

The next administrative level of the bank's operation is an area office, which supervises ten branches. Ten area offices constitute a zonal office. The zonal offices are managed by the head office which is situated in the capital city, Dhaka. Each branch of the bank borrows money from the head office at 12% and on lends it to borrowers at 20%. The branch office is supposed to cover all its costs from the 8% margin; after three to four years of operation, the branch usually starts making profit. One or two Zonal Manager Conferences are held in the head office every year:

A Conference lasts for three days and all Zonal Managers participate-one area manager from each zone and all department and section heads from the head office, including the managing director, deputy managing director and general managers. Usually zonal audit officers are also invited to attend these all important meetings. Under the supervision of the managing directors, participants discuss the critical issues facing the bank. Many of the major decisions, such as those involving the introduction of new products, the development of important policy, and rule changes, are made in these meetings. The meetings are also used to hammer out differences on major policy and implementation issues across zones.

Its loan program includes basic loan, housing loan, and higher education loan for member's children, micro enterprise loan, loan for village phone, business loan for graduate students of Grameen families and loan for struggling members. Grameen has also life and loan insurance products. The period for the basic loan may vary from 3 months to 3 years. The period for housing loan is 10 years. Micro enterprise loan is also given for a period up to 3 years, education loan provided for the period of education. Grameen has also scholarship program for the children of its members. The basic loan which includes all income generating loan activities constitutes about 98 percent of the total loan portfolio.

The first disbursement of Grameen loan was US$ 27 to 42 members. The cumulative disbursement by the end of September 2008 stood at US $ 7.4 billion. The monthly disbursement is more than US $ 80 million. The amount of loan outstanding was US $ 609.60 million in September 2008. Grameen has different kinds of savings products.

These are Grameen Pension Savings (for Grameen Bank members and staff), personal savings (open to all), double in 7years-term deposits (open to all), loan insurance savings fund (Grameen Bank members), Fixed Deposit with monthly income (open to all) and others (like weekly compulsory saving at the rate of taka 10, additional GPS etc.). Grameen has mobilized more than US$ 826 million as deposits including US$ 373 from non-members (Sept. 2008).

The deposit as percentage of outstanding loans is 136 percent. Grameen Bank offers very attractive rates for deposits. Minimum interest offered is 8.5 percent and maximum rate is 12 percent. As Grameen is always for developing and operating a sustainable micro credit program, it charges the borrowers an affordable interest rate. It remains cautions to avoid changing a price which makes the borrowers pay for any inefficiency of the system or luxury of its management.

According to Professor Muhammad Yunus poverty focused microcredit programs should charge a lower rate of interest which may be equal to the cost of funds at the market rate plus up to 10 percent. He calls it Green Zone. It may be in the Yellow Zone as well which equals the cost of funds plus 10 to 15 percent. If any program charges an interest rate higher than the Yellow Zone, they operate in the Red Zone, which according to Professor Muhammad

Yunus is the territory of the moneylenders. This is for maximizing profit and not for maximizing social benefit.

The interest rate Grameen Bank charges for its loans is lower than the rate of interest the government of Bangladesh has fixed for government run microcredit programs. The interest rate for government program is 11 percent flat. It is only 10 percent flat for Grameen basic loans.

There are in fact four interest rates for loans from Grameen Bank: 20 percent (declining basis) for income generating loans, 8 percent for housing loan, 5 percent for student loan and interest free loans for struggling members who are beggars. All interests are simple interest. The amount collected from the borrowers in interest can never exceed the principal amount.

Inspiring Principles

The most innovative aspect of microcredit experience is the focus on developmental principles of individuals.

a) Trust based credit
b) Women
c) The group and its potentials
d) From charity to credit
e) From theory to practice
f) The value of self-employment

The Trust

People receive loans on trust. When a person goes to a bank to apply for a loan to start an economical activity, real guarantees are asked. A poor person does not own anything, thus has got no chance to get out of its status of poverty.

Yunus started his venture giving money to poor people on trust thus setting up an extraordinary innovation. Loaning money on trust, indeed, establishes a real "reversal" of the logic of traditional credit. Yunus claims that the poor knows that the credit is his only chance, beyond which they have no alternatives, and that's why he won't throw away the only chance he's being given.

Yunus' will was to contrast the prejudices against poor lending them money without asking for any material guarantee. The real guarantee was their creativity and their commitment.

After 30 years from the beginning of this experiment the overall balance is formidable: 7.000.000 are the beneficiaries that received a loan and have consequently become members of the Bank. The repayment rate exceeds 99% and on 95% of cases they are women.

The Women

In Bangladesh, says Yunus, the women are living the dramatic experience of not being able to feed their children in times of penury and famine. For this duty, so fundamental of their identity, women appear to be more reliable and able to "generate development", because when the projects are managed by them, you obtain the best beneficial effects on the families.

This is what happened in the region of Kerala in India where, during the study on Human Development Index, it was pointed out how the parameters of life expectancy are comparable to those in the countries with high income thanks to the cultural level of women, their ability to raise the children to which they convey forms of self care that they can bring with them through a long lasting life. Moreover they have a peculiar attention towards the environment and its preservation that can be obtained through the comprehension of the ecological dynamics acquired thanks to a good education. Thus women are two extraordinary sources for development, being source on their own and also educator of the future generations.

The Group and its Potentials

When the poor finds himself acting on his own he feels like he's exposed to any kind of risks. Feeling as a part of a group, instead, makes him feel a sense of safety that puts him in the conditions to face the risk tasks necessary to start an enterprise.

From Charity to Credit

Generally we don't realize that, often, a charitable attitude leads to donate those two pennies in the street, so that the poor disappears from our sight and drifts away. Probably I am not conscious about that, but his presence embarrasses me, sets in me a problem, a conflict and annoys me. A donation of money, often, as an automatism ad with no awareness, implies a demand for the beggar to disappear and relieve the embarrassment and the problem.

It's a widespread mechanism that operates both on an individual level, and with international aid. Yunus, indeed, claims that there should be an "International Authority" that would take care of phenomena that, with the declared intention of helping the development, cause poverty and increase the inequalities between "developed" countries and "developing" countries.

From Theory to Practice

Yunus always felt a kind of thrill while explaining to his students at University that the economical theories where able to give answers to any kind of economical problems. However, he tells he started to feel a sense of emptiness. Asking him what were worth all of those nice theories if people kept on dying from starvation under the bridges and on the streets.

It's in that occasion that Yunus organizes training with some of the students of his university course in Chittagong, his birth place. He proposed to go in an extremely poor village close to the city where he proposed to make a list of the things necessary to the inhabitants of that village in order to survive for one week to the famine the country was going through, without being blackmailed by usurers.

He realized that 50 dollars were sufficient, and he given them from his pocket. That's how he started his adventure, with an act of trust and generosity, what every enterprise needs.

The Value of Self Employment

An independent job gives to a person a wider range of possibilities of influencing his own destiny and the work itself, right through the satisfaction that we always feel facing our work in which we see sense, meaning, utility and development in the exchange, returns and strengthens an identity that gets lost and crushed in an employee job atomized by industrial enterprises in the assembly line. In the category of independent jobs are included the small craftsman, the small trade, the services and other forms of creative expressions.

Social Rules and the XVI Decisions

When we talk about micro-credit it is clear that it does not represent only a quantitative concept but a qualitative one as well. It is based, in fact, on the idea that poverty is perpetrated through formal and informal rules and values that implicitly maintain the economical and social asset, which keeps those people in a status of poverty. This is especially evident if we are looking at the sixteen decisions that every beneficiary of the Grameen bank as to sign.

Grameen Bank's 16 Decisions are an example of a social development program melded with microcredit delivery. They were developed in a 1984 workshop of Grameen Bank members representing 100 Centres, and have been an integral part of Grameen Bank's mission ever since.

The decisions are:

1. The four principles of the Grameen Bank - Discipline, Unity, Courage and Hard Work - we shall follow and advance in all walks of our lives.
2. Prosperity we shall bring to our families.
3. We shall not live in dilapidated houses. We shall repair our houses and work towards constructing new houses at the earliest.
4. We shall grow vegetables all the year around. We shall eat plenty of them and sell the surplus.
5. During the planting seasons, we shall plant as many seedlings as possible.
6. We shall plan to keep our families small. We shall minimize our expenditures. We shall look after our health.
7. We shall educate our children and ensure that they can earn to pay for their education.
8. We shall always keep our children and the environment clean.
9. We shall build and use pit-latrines.
10. We shall drink tube-well water. If it is not available, we shall boil water or use alum.
11. We shall not take any dowry in our sons' weddings; neither shall we give any dowry in our daughters' weddings. We shall keep the Center free from the curse of dowry. We shall not practice child marriage.
12. We shall not inflict any injustice on anyone; neither shall we allow anyone to do so.
13. For higher income, we shall collectively undertake bigger investments.
14. We shall always be ready to help each other. If anyone is in difficulty, we shall all help them.
15. If we come to know of any breach of discipline in any Center, we shall al go there and help restore discipline.
16. We shall introduce physical exercise in all our Centers. We shall take part in all social activities collectively.

As we can see we talk of rules which are inner and outer and involve individuals, families and social context and also their intertwining. In other words, we are talking of the quality of social relations.

Microcredit is not a small credit, but a great developmental process to eradicate poverty that functions on a small steps policy. It is a medium-long term process that implies the real participation of the population involved as you cannot oblige people to do a microcredit experience.

In his work, Yunus has tried to individuate those rules that implicitly maintain poverty in the Bengali society and all Grameen Bank beneficiaries have been asked to subscribe, previously, some rules created with the purpose to interrupt the vicious circle.

This is a sort of articulated social agreement by which all beneficiaries accept to undermine those rules that create obstacles for the development of the whole Grameen Community.

For example, the obligation that parents have to pay for each daughter's dowry for their marriage often drains all family resources and, as a consequence, the birth of a girl becomes a sort of despair for the whole family, creating a bad attitude towards women.

Microcredit offers women the opportunities to re-gain a role of being individuals producing resources inside the family and the Community.

The process applies to individuals and their mirroring to social rules in spite of the damages that potentially derives to them from those rules. In fact, what seems to be strange and difficult to understand is the sense of inability that they share with the social recognition and status that they receive.

In the context of psycho-relational development, such an attitude in the child/mother relationship is seen and understood as a relation that is unable to develop children abilities and it is diagnosed in the frame of a dismissing mother. We try to transpose this concept to another context and talk here of a kind of dismissing social mother community, unable to give value to her children-citizens.

The Grameen Model and its Efficacy on Tangible and Intangible Goods

Both tangible and intangible aspects are always present in all exchange and in life in general as an expression of a relational system, in which we all live.

What is special and innovative in microcredit is the value given to both aspects, aiming at an idea of human being as "not one-dimensional entities, they are excitingly multi-dimensional entities and indeed very colorful. Their emotions, beliefs, priorities, behavior patterns vary so much that they can be more aptly described by drawing analogy with producing millions of colors and shades by mixing three basic colors in varying proportions (Yunus, 2006).

Microcredit, in fact, can be described as a tool for development based on "relational goods" and "microcredit operators" know, or should know the importance of taking into consideration both parts of it: "bread and roses".

They are in equal parts essential for the creation and the development of microcredit and for the development of persons themselves.

We can represent microcredit graphically in a figure 1 that somehow shows a continuum. On the graphic's extremes we have, on one side concrete, tangible outcomes, and on the other side, relations.

The tangible and intangible dimension interrelate and we could even say that money, the concreteness, can be seen as a pretext for the whole experience, which becomes "special" and "rich" only by reaching the best intertwining of these two aspects.

The setting, that is the practical "instrument" in which the relational frame is structured, can be organized in many ways. It can have on one side, the concrete dimension - in figure - and on the other one, the intangible, as the ground or vice versa.

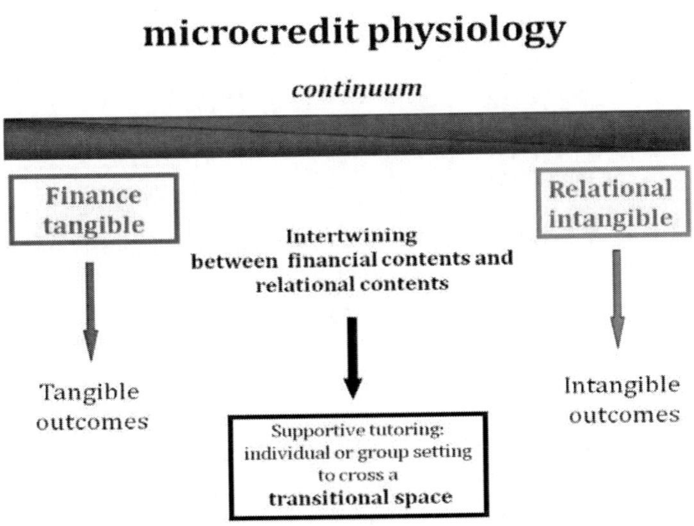

Figure 1. Microcredit physiology.

MC, in this representation is seen as a tool for development; which is the starting point depends on the population and specific context, and both definitions and interactions will determine the blending of these two sides and the allocation of the experience in the continuum described.

Some research findings show that the more relational engagement is offered by microcredit Officers, the higher is the repayment rate. It is a matter of whether to invest in one or in the other one of the two sides of the whole.

Of course, "*in medio stat virtus*".

In the Grameen experience, one hundred per cent of the whole is reached and a great deal of relational commitment is offered.

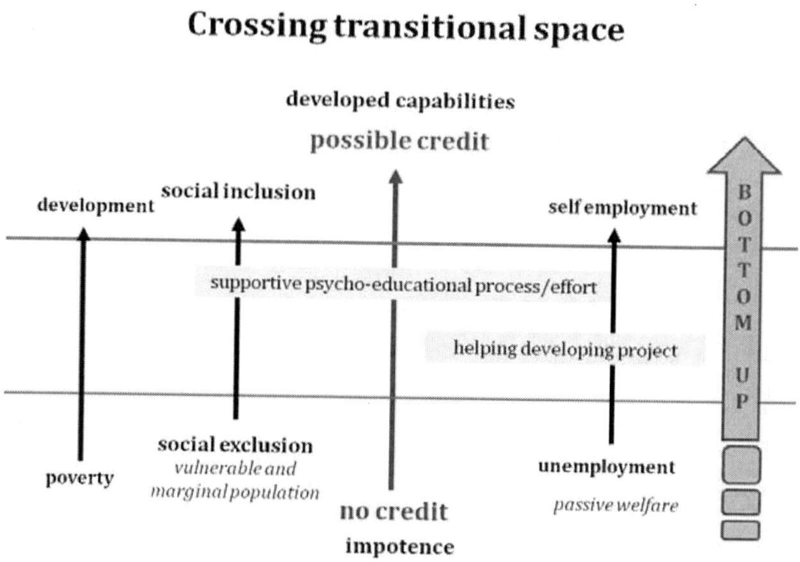

Figure 2. Crossing transitional space.

Sometimes a certain excess of social pressure is created in groups' relations, so that beneficiaries tend to become more than overwhelmed by the debt. This is often a consequence of the group conductor's inability. He has to be a professional, a specialist able to blend both sides of the matter: money and relations.

So we can say that relations are both fuel and aim of the whole matter and show how "human sustainability" is crucial for this kind of development.

It could probably be argued that from a financial point of view, the experience is not sustainable, but what makes it become sustainable, at the end of the day, is the human and social aspect of it all. This implies that practical counting should include wider sets of figures than usual like, for example, the social costs implied, spent or saved in the whole experience.

Another concept which plays an important role is what we define here as "transitional space", which is strongly based on the relational aspects of the MC experience.

By transitional space we mean a process of change that, starting from a situation in which poor people feel impotence and despair, they can transform these feelings into hope and possibility. This process takes place mainly through the help of supportive psycho-educational relations specialized in filling the gap between impotence and possibility, between absence of credit and possibility to have it.

Inner Poverty, Intra-Psychic Poverty

The feeling of "nowhere", nothing, impotence is what I name as "inner poverty". In clinical individual terms, we can also call it depression. But in this case we shouldn't take into consideration the possible socio-economical reasons for it. From studies of human development we know that a baby who has no possibility to relate to another human being will stop willing to live and dies by what is called "cachexia". What is necessary for a baby to reach the "tit" of the mother is the will to do so. What is necessary for sucking the "tit" for a baby is the desire to do so; and in doing so, the baby transforms the desire of milk into a possibility to live both physically and psychologically. The psychology of poverty is characterized by a sense of emptiness, of "no value" and lack of "object investment": that becomes lack of investment on oneself as a "self object". This is the psychological area in which the process takes place: no value is given to me; no value can I offer to myself, no value can I give back to anyone, including Society and Community as I did not receive any relational consistency in my early development stages. Through these mechanisms it is possible to understand how social reasons for poverty can become inner, subjective reasons and also effects of it. Offering money on trust, which is what Grameen Bank does, is a demonstration to be a trustable person that can trust thy self as well. This is how the process of increasing (better said creating) self esteem starts and allows these persons to take the risk to confront with the reality of their capabilities. Usually the process is virtuous and, in case of failure, no punishment is given as it is meant to be included in the possible losses. And, in any case, the effort of Grameen is to try to avoid exclusion, offering other possibilities for repayment, and in this way avoiding the development of shame in those who have not been able to succeed.

Shame and Poverty

Shame is another aspect of poverty: an inner feeling that corresponds to a sense of humiliation facing the comparison to others who, by definition, are "more" or "better". This feeling can contribute to a process of depleting the value of inner resources that, again by definition, are "less" or "worst". These emotions turn very easily into a sense of impotence and humiliation, which themselves become rage and violence.

The aim of microcredit is the opposite: to transform shame into pride.

Poverty, "New Poverty" and Social Exclusion

What has been expressed in relation to poverty for developing countries can be repeated, "mutatis mutandis", for what concerns social exclusion in the so called "developed" countries.

In these countries people do not die for the lack of food but "die" metaphorically for the lack or insufficiency of social links and social life. Exclusion and deviancy that often arise from those difficult situations are the result of social struggles people play every day.

Social exclusion, in fact, corresponds to poverty in terms of relations, both social and economical. The consequences for individuals and families are very painful and people can develop great suffering inside themselves and, at the same time, they can produce great difficulties in social life for the Community itself, in terms of social wellbeing, "social mirroring" and security. The same process of facing unbearable comparison to "more lucky others" becomes humiliation and shame, leading to the possibility of transforming these painful emotions into rage and violence and, consequently into deviancy.

Social exclusion, besides the ethical concerns, produces great costs to Society, which could be re-arranged facing a new vision of the welfare system, more oriented towards the development of resources instead of humiliating and "expensive" charitable attitudes (ways of functioning). The philosophy implied is that the resources people can offer to Society should be seen as a loss for the whole Community whenever it is not possible to develop them into something good for all, through creativity and diffused social trust.

CONCLUSION

When a "poor person" starts the microcredit experience, he or she has to learn many things and this is not the main problem, because he or she has to "learn how to learn". In fact, he has to overcome many obstacles, internal and external, interpersonal and socio-cultural. Some of them have to do with inner space and beliefs and those parts of the identity that reflect socio cultural rules that keep these people in a state of poverty.

Other obstacles play a role in terms of the identity of those other people who are used to relate to the poor. They need to change their mental representation and consequent behavior.

A difficulty, at the beginning, was to understand the great "revolutionary strength" of microcredit for the development of common people. Handling business and developing resources is not such an easy task for those who have been used to think that "they are not allowed to be able to do anything". I should go further than this idea of being able.

In fact, in general, for these people, the possibility to do something does not even come to their mind. It is, as I said previously, unthinkable because poverty is the reason and the result of a disvalued personal and cultural identity. This is the problem, or at least part of it and one of them.

REFERENCES

Yunus, M. (1974). *Three Farmers of Jobra*; Department of Economics, Chittagong University.

Yunus, M. (1994). *Grameen Bank, as I See it*; Dhaka: Grameen Bank.

Yunus, M. (1997). *Vers un monde sans pauvreté*. Paris: Éditions Jean-Claude Lattès.

Yunus, M. (2007). Credit for the poor: poverty as a distant history. *Harvard International Review, Vol.29, no.3*, pp. 20-24.

Yunus, M. (2008). *Creating a World without Poverty: Social Business and the Future of Capitalism*. Ney York: Public Affairs.

Yunus, M. (2010). *Building Social Business: The New Kind of Capitalism that Serves Humanity's Most Pressing Needs*. New York: Public Affairs.

In: The Other Side of the Coin
Editors: L. Brunori and M. Pines
ISBN: 978-1-62618-726-9

Chapter 2

THE ECONOMY OF THE GROUP

***Luisa Brunori*[*] *and Chiara Bleve*[†]**
Department of Psychology, University of Bologna

ABSTRACT

Oikôs nomos, the Greek expression from which the word 'economy' originates, means the 'management of the family home'. This takes us to the idea of a good system of sharing not only in the Family but also in the Community and in the Society as well.

In this paper, the psychological point of view meets the economical side to describe the practice of Grameen Microcredit model. Microcredit, in fact, is an intertwining system between tangible and intangible aspects that are blended in a very special virtuous way.

Muhammad Yunus, the founder of microcredit, has put the group at the centre of the whole Microcredit experience. The methodology is concentrated in a process of change: *"from when I was unable to towards the possibility to be able to from now on"*.

The practice of this process is clearly oriented towards offering to these people, besides the loan, the right of human beings, the recognition of their value for their community and the dignity of citizens. In this way each person is able to contribute to the community's needs through their capabilities. The group situation can be seen as a transitional space where

[*] Correspondence regarding this chapter may be addressed to Luisa Brunori *luisa.brunori@unibo.it* and
[†] Chiara Bleve, *chiara.bleve@unibo.it*.

the trust is like a necessary ingredient in the whole process. We consider microcredit as a bottom-up process, based on trust and on relational goods.

INTRODUCTION

In this chapter we attempt to propose an organic connection between certain elements of the relational economy and group analytic theory as it is described in the treatments of Elias (1999), Foulkes (1983), Pines (1968;1978;1981) and other colleagues, active scholars and researchers within this discipline.

Group analysis is an approach of dynamic psychology which focuses on the group dimension as the place for the creation of the psyche. According to this perspective, individuals are shaped through a continuous and dynamic interweaving between themselves and the original group, the family, and then following through the next sub-groups until the larger group dimension of the polis, the place of *civis* individual recognition, full-fledged participant of *oikòs nomos*.

The individual is, at the same time, subject and part of the community. One part cannot be separated from the other. It can instead be identified by imagining one in a central position, as a figure, while the other is on the background and vice versa. The Moebius strip can represent this continuum.

It is not surprising that this theoretical approach is particularly "suited" to collect a deep connection between psychology and economics, especially when you consider the etymological meaning of the word *oikòs - nomos* which contains, and at the same time, is built on a relational meaning: the rule of the house, the rule that governs the parties involved.

The micro-credit, a practice that in its original version is based on group relations, is a particularly interesting case study for this consideration.

EFFECTIVENESS AND EFFICIENCY OF THE GROUP

A first reflection on the cost effectiveness of the groups arises from the question of the effectiveness and efficiency of psychotherapies.

Since the nineties, in fact, as far as the area of the "*managed care system*"[1] is concerned, the key issue arising was to identifying the "best health practices."

The need to evaluate the outcome of interventions was obviously highly relevant.

In 1989, Volker Tschuschke, from the University of Cologne, published a research on the compared evaluation of the effectiveness and efficiency of group psychotherapies and individual psychotherapies. This analysis compared the results of the clinical application of the group analytic technique in individual and group settings.

From the results of Volker Tschuschke (1989) study, it was found that, from the point of view of efficiency, individual therapy and group therapy obtained similar results. From the point of view of efficiency, however, group psychotherapy obtained more advantageous results.

The proportion was 1 to 13 compared with a numerical relationship therapist-patient of 1 to 7/8. To understand this value, the prospect of saving resources was not enough, or rather a therapist for seven patients the members of the group. Instead, it was necessary to understand what the residues five points meant equivalent to the wage in relation to the value of thirteen.

An in-depth study has shown that, thirty months after the end of the therapy, a series of behaviors, seen as the expression of a strong dependency needs (hospitalization, specialist and / or general checks done without a substantial medical necessity), were significantly lower for those who had received psychotherapy group compared to those who had attended individual psychotherapy.

Researchers at the school of Cologne have interpreted this result as an expression of an added value, specific of the group psychotherapy, and they recognized in the group a tool that can more easily develop forms of autonomy, self-management, equal social skills in individuals who taken part in.

A possible explanation is related to the specific technique of the "group analytic" group.

As a matter of facts, within the clinical practice, the participants in a therapeutic group benefit from an experimental and protected situation, thanks to what in the jargon is called "*ego training in action*". Here, everyone can

---

[1] The concept of *managed care* refers to every form of health care that tries to check the costs of the offered service proposed by MacKenzie 1995.

recognize their more or less conscious relational modalities, through exchange and dialogue.

They can also identify their "favorite ones" and be able to acquire the necessary self-control to choose, to settle, and to make sense of themselves, their own problems and to help others, in a form that gives back self-esteem and transforms the feeling of helplessness in one of power; a kind of training to relations through a continuous experimentation.

The autonomy of the patients is intended as a goal achieved through an arduous and challenging process of individuation-separation and development work carried out by others, and through others.

Self-management, responsibility, the mirroring process as the recognition of others similar to us in needs and desires, but different in history and representation of the world are fundamental basic elements of a process that helps to find an interior "wellbeing" subjective and social at the same time.

Further reflections allowed us to conclude that what a psychotherapy group oriented to group analysis can offer to its patients is an added value that has to do with an increase of patients' ability to flourish as entrepreneurs of themselves, able to develop what Sen (1985) calls "capabilities". This link, so closely connected with economic concepts, led us to coin the term of cost effectiveness of the group" since the group is able to develop individuals at their best, generating benefits for each of them and for the community.

These considerations give us the idea that a group has cost effectiveness if we conceive it in the sense of relational structure with high potential, and therefore able to produce "relational goods" which, by definition, are based on equal relationships centered on reciprocity and shared responsibilities.

To ensure that, it's necessary to preserve a strong group identity aspect, what we call "condition of unstable equilibrium"[2]. It is a dynamic dynamism that is accomplished through a continuous influence among the different parts: a process of change theoretically infinite that produces a number of theoretically infinite relational exchanges.

In order for this to happen, it is necessary that the group identifies itself in a model that can trigger values and relationships based on diversity and multiplicity. This will be able to develop democracy, trust, altruism, individual autonomy and responsibility inside the group.

The quality of leadership is crucial, and the risk, where lacking the necessary skills, is to generate totally opposite group dynamics that tend to

[2] In physics, unstable equilibrium is a particular case of static equilibrium and mechanical equilibrium in which a minimum solicitation can change the condition of equilibrium and to make to collapse the system.

uniqueness, the *reductio ad unum* of a process so complex and powerful. The scapegoat is one of them.

Points of Convergence between Group Analysis and Economics: The Meaning of Cost Effectiveness

During a symposium held in Venice in 2002 by the Group Analytic Society (GAS) with the University of Bologna on the theme of the symbolic meaning of money and the money linked to the relationships between people, we were surprised to recognize some particularly relevant similarities between concepts of civil economy and theoretical content of group analysis.

This led to a long reflection on the meaning of these coincidences that allowed us to better define the cost effectiveness of the group[3] as a multidisciplinary concept.

The etymology of "economic" comes from the Greek "*oikos nomos*": "the rule of the house"; the good family man's rule.

We can therefore define a group as economic where and if it is able to enhance the parts of which it is composed by, thus increasing its internal dynamics and relationships as intended in their sense of resources that are created in the group itself through a continuous exchange.

It is clear that this concept is not referring to the idea of cost savings or shortage; vice versa as the possibility of expressing group elements of plurality and diversity recognized and recognizable as resources developed and accepted within the group.

To identify within relationships an economic meaning, it is to point out the rule that holds them together.

For the psychologists' community, the relationships represent the basis for any considerations about the development of the individual. The relational paradigm, independently from the different theoretical points of view, constitutes a strong and irreplaceable element, in relation to the construction of the person, and it is acquired universally, well established within the scientific community.

The intra-psychic relational structure and relational models culturally and socially acquired are founding and fundamental aspects of individuals.

---

[3] Acts of the conference The economy of the group. Relational Goods in society, mind and brain, Venice, 2002.

The integration between economics and psychology is possible if we start from the concept of relational goods as a bridge between the two disciplines.

Other points of convergence are issues such as solidarity, cooperation, reciprocity, democracy and altruism.

It could be argued that group analysis discovers relationships as assets and the civilian economy rediscovers the goods in relationships.

In such a framework, relations can be imagined as commodities that produce and originate other relational goods.

The wellbeing of a community and thus of its individuals is directly proportional to the amount of communication and exchange that it is possible to create. The greater is the possibility of each one to take part in the life of the Community, the more economic is the situation created.

Then, the concept of cost effectiveness proves to be an attribution of value to social participation.

Why We Call Them Relational Goods

Carole Uhlaner (1989), which made an important contribution to the study of relational goods by inventing the expression, wrote that "relational goods are goods that can only be owned through mutual agreements that are in place after appropriate joint actions undertaken by a person and not from other arbitrary [...] the goods that occur in trade where everyone can provide it anonymously are not relational."(Uhlaner, 1989; p. 254)

The people identity is thus central for the production of such goods.

Relational goods can neither be produced nor consumed alone, and therefore cannot be acquired in a solitary way, because they depend on interactions with others and are created and can be enjoyed only if shared. Their essential characteristic is that they require reciprocity and cannot be pursued independently from of the choices of the people involved.

Examples of relational goods are, according to the author, social approval, solidarity, friendship, sense of belonging to a particular group, as well as identification with its rules. Uhlaner's argument stems from the recognition that the traditional models of "rational choice" cannot explain certain behaviors.

An example that the author proposes regarding this topic is the participation in elections where it is not clear why individuals are willing to incur costs to go to vote when they know that the influence of their vote on the final results is almost nil. The situation changes if we consider the fact that an important dimension of the vote is to define the identity through the relationship with the community that comes true in this circumstance, through participation in a social event.

In this case, economical costs for going to vote seem no longer so irrational, as the vote provides a good in social terms, which is the constitution of personal identity that, as previously discussed, cannot be achieved privately.

Therefore, not only the final good itself, but also the process from which this generated, as well as the ways through which it is delivered, acquire value. Zamagni (2002)[4] explains, in this regard, that the motivation to participate in the production of relational goods cannot be external to the relationship, but it is created between the members themselves: the value of these goods varies according to the key players of the exchange.

For a better understanding, we use a further concept that helps us in opposition that describes the positional goods.

The positional goods, by definition, involve an unequal distribution between individuals; they placed people in a vertical stratification, and are not affected by the identity of the person, because the position on the vertical of power is what counts.

In other words, where the free, equal and reciprocal friendship is the prototype of relational goods, the status symbol is one of the most representative examples of positional goods, as it is consumed as a substitute for real status, and used in its meaning of symbol to signify a desired location in the social stratification.

Far from intention to create simplified type good/bad, where relational goods are good and positional goods are bad, it is possible to depict them as opposite ends of a continuum in which to imagine the social relational system as a whole starting from individuals.

In every circumstance, everyone will opt for a relational code of a type with the other in the background and vice versa as it is intuitive to understand that organisms and relational circumstances will be better characterized by either mode; however, the other will always be present in a plot of figure ground as both locations do not exist in the "pure" state, but they interact continuously establishing prevalence in one way or another.

---

[4] During the conference "The economy of the group. Relational Goods in society, mind and brain", Venice, 2002.

Group Conditions That Facilitate the Development of Cost Effectiveness

In order to argue that the group has cost effectiveness, according to the meaning of the development of resources previously described, some specific relational conditions are necessary inside it to generate among its members: trust, altruism and democracy. Psychologists consider trust as the main ingredient of the original relationship between mother and child for a "healthy development." However, if trust is essential during the early stages, its presence is no less important in the subsequent ones for relationships within secondary groups that we experience in our daily social life, outside the family. Precisely because they represent a continuous and constant reinforcement of our personal and social original identity, they represent the habitat of living with our fellow men, the place of the expression of citizenship. Trust is seen, in this sense, as a basic tool for maintaining the mental health of human beings, the trust thanks to which citizens are entitled to state that we live in a civilized society in which exchange reciprocity, responsibility and justice in social relations and to generate vital energy and hope, necessary in a plan of a "healthy" and productive life.

Even for a good economy, as Fukuyama (1995) says that trust is an essential ingredient.

In saying this, the author recognizes the social virtues, among which trust is the principal, the basis for the creation of prosperity, the reduction in transactions costs and social development, simultaneously, a capital that enriches the entire Community.

In addition to trust, even altruism contributes to develop cost effectiveness if intended as an acknowledgement of others' reality and the ability to recognize themselves simply as one among others.

We return with this statement to the concept of "mirroring process"[5], whose neurological bases are the subject of recent extraordinary neuro-physiological discoveries: the "mirror neurons"[6].

---

[5] The mirroring process has been defined by Pines (1983) as something belonging to others that evokes proper insides elements and this allows to look at them.

[6] The new discoveries of the neuroscientists of the Laboratory of the University in Parma (Rizzolatti, 2003) see in the neuronal structures the social basis we are talking about through the individualization of the so called "neurons mirror": they are cortical neurons multimodal able to be activated by different sensorial modalities "reflecting" the actions of the others. More precisely, they are neurons that behave as the motor neurons when they are activated for a proper action, while they are showing their own peculiarity when they are activated in answer to the same action completed by others.

Mind and brain express in this way, the need and similar instruments for the realization of the exchange as the essence of relational life or even of life itself.

In addition to the elements described, democracy is as the expression of a harmonious system of relational diversity, understood as sharing of norms and values that enable cooperation, mutual growth and benefit sharing.

Democracy implies in fact a deep respect for everyone's needs and the consequent recognition of value in diversity and multiplicity, in support of the development of the emotional and social capital.

Multiplicity and Uniqueness

We have defined the group as "a high-powered relational structure" provided that it is safeguarded plurality. The opposite occurs when the single thought takes over.

The "single thought", as indicated by Stiglitz (1990), is to the economic system as authoritarianism is to the economy of the group. Authoritarianism, in fact, does not allow the development of the resources around it, unless they are copies of itself.

The single thought expresses an authoritarian and self-referential concept, which refers to a structure where, by definition, what is different, is excluded and only the vertical aspects of relationships are endorsed. Through the *reductio ad unum,* every possible and various aspect of reality and social reality accepted in this case is reduced to a single defined form. The consequences of this condition, lead to a reduction of the potential space for creative and divergent solutions and an exasperation of social marginalization. To accept the thoughts of everyone means to accept the plurality and diversity by expressing the most of the group cost effectiveness, where relationships are "n^n" and where there is the coexistence of so many different ideas.

The problem that arises here is how to "manage" these differences and how to navigate through the *mare magnum* of so many resources.

Horizontality and Verticality

Each group as a social aggregate, from the family onward, contains all the institutional elements that collect both reality data and specific cultural interpretation and proposal of coexistence among its members.

It is in this diversity that horizontal and vertical elements are intertwined.

In the primary family group the parents, the authority, the trans-generational are placed on the vertical line, while the brothers are on the horizontal one. Similarly, in the secondary groups, it is the master, the professor, the boss who supports the verticality, while classmates, playmates and colleagues endorse the horizontal one.

The relational consequences and the configurations that take place in the relations within the group, changed very substantially if it prevails one or the other mode. We must not forget that this plot is the supporting structure of the group.

The value of one or the other and their interaction figure / ground is what makes the difference where, again, one is in the protagonist position of "figure" and the other is background and vice versa.

Even the subjects' aptitude which takes part in different way in the group, plays in theory an important role: the ways in which each individual has developed the group intra-psychically and brings it forward in relationships are endless. In terms of group analysis, we could talk about *foundation matrix*[7] of each individual and "dynamic matrix" of the group as an elaboration of the plot of all relational and transferal contents of the individuals.

In the clinical application of the group analysis technique, and by disciplinary convention, two words are employed to describe the vertical / horizontal plot and their different increasing value: the change in the group and through the group.

In the first case [Fig.3] the links highlighted are those that occur between each member and the leader of the group and the vertical relational aspect prevails.

The group centered on the conductor (C) generates necessarily rivalry towards the object more valued that, in the specific case, is the authority figure that, being unique for all, is also poor.It could even be argued that the group is structured through a series of "couples" between each member and the conductor.

---

[7] "The matrix is the hypothetical web of communication and relationship in a given group. It is the common shared ground which ultimately determines the meaning and significance of all events and upon which all communication and interpretations, verbal and non-verbal rest" (Foulkes 1964).

In this particular case, the basic matrix is "what enables communication within a particular ethnic group, common substrate whose presence allows the immediate mutual understanding;" the dynamic matrix "is built within the group situation as a peculiar fact towards a particular group, representing the view of what is happening "here" and "now" in terms of even unconscious communication." (Di Maria, Formica, 2009, p.95-96).

Keeping the comparison/parallelism with the economic sphere, this is a group based on the concept of positional goods where the desired position is represented by the proximity to the authority or to the most appreciated extreme of the vertical.

The second case [Fig.4] shows all possible relationships between the different members included the conductor. It is visible here as the horizontal relational aspect prevails; this is based on the fact that every relationship is an exchange that produces knowledge of self and others, and it is enriched by the inclusion of diversity and multiplicity. This is the group of reciprocity and relational goods.

It should be noted that the group forms we are talking about/that are being discussed occur naturally within the social system in which each of us live. As previously mentioned, infinite processes are generated in all groups; these are related both to vertical as well as horizontal relationships. The difference lies in the management of the group and in the *raison d'être* of the group. Depending on the goals that are to be achieved, some relational aspects rather than others will be used. It is a matter of a mental representation of the group by each member on the basis of familiar and cultural acquisitions as a social construction of mind: the matrix.

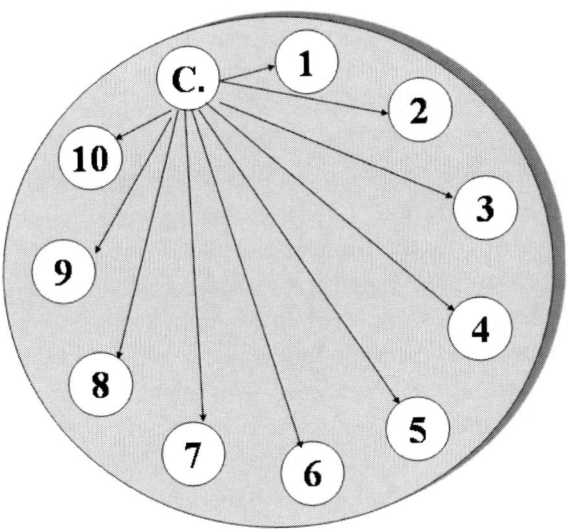

Figure 3. Vertical relational aspect.

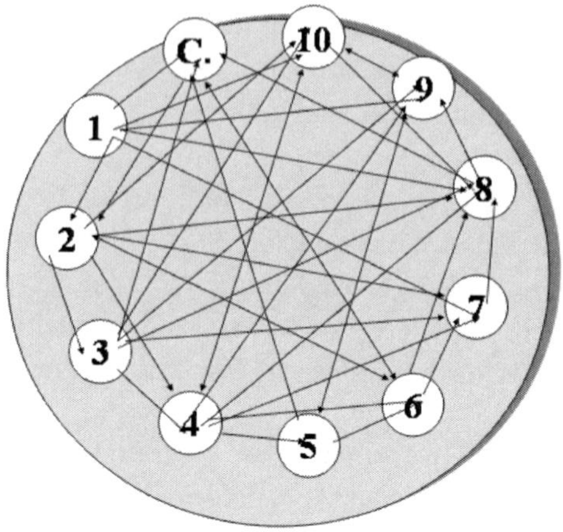

Figure 4. horizontal relational aspect.

MECHANISMS OF COST EFFECTIVENESS AND "DISECONOMY"

The etymon of "group" comes from "tangle", "knot" but also from "crop", "bolus", the "part of bird's neck, bladder-shaped, where food stops."[8] In this sense, the bolus refers to something that, chewed and mixed with saliva, loses the identity of the individual parts which is composed by: it becomes something else.

As mentioned above, the group is a place of exchanges, mirroring process, resonances, and the interaction of dynamic change and an unstable equilibrium for each individual and for the group as a whole.

Focusing back to the psychotherapy group, as a conceptual place for our reflection, the group, as a clinical tool for individuals, represents an object invested with hope but at the same time, threats. While individual participants can take help in sharing the experience with others, on the other hand, until then unexpected and unknown feelings may arise in relation to others.

The hypothesis, on which this practice is based on, is the individual participants can get help in sharing their experience of working memory with

[8] The definition of "bolus" has been translated from the D.Olivieri, 1953. Dizionario etimologico italiano, Ceschina, Milano.

others and the search for assignment of a new meaning to their suffering, to their lives.

This process request each participant to bring their psychic contents to the group that will be understood, processed and transformed through the continuous exchange in the group, as previously described. These elements will be returned later on to each one enriched by the development that the group as a whole as well as each member will be able to achieve.

Obviously, hope and fear of change are the emotional elements which would be continuously/always present in this process.

They are personal private ancient and profound contents, basic elements of the people which will intertwine and turn into this group melting pot made up of cognitive and emotional elements, subjective and social at the same time.

It is a place of confluence of social and individual content, cognitive and emotional aspects of everyone, a place able to develop and contain deep regressive tensions and to produce exchange, maturation and growth. The group is the result of the fact that each individual brings their own content, which is intertwined with those of others, thus creating new alchemy. Everything gets back to each individual through these relationships and helps to create a new image and conformation of oneself.

The way through which the group comes up with the duality individual-group when some situations do not allow the group to express itself in the form of mutual benefit between the parties is crucial in this reflection. In other words, within these circumstances the dynamics that hinder the expression of the multiplicity prevail and are inclined to generate exclusion.

The scapegoat is the most common among these mechanisms and it is characterized by the concentration of aggressive contents of the group against one of its members preventing, thus, the group from developing such aggressiveness.

The Monopolist, however, centralizes on himself most of the space, the attention, the time of the group and hampers so the exchange and the growth because he limits the expression of others.

An excess of conformity prevents the expression of differences and tends to create what is called "massified[9]" or "agglutinate group" in its most regressive form.

The conflict between the group and individuals is physiological and natural and the resolution to this conflict is what makes the difference in social relationships.

---

[9] i.e. depersonalized

Where individual and group are engaged in a zero-sum relationship[10], one will be the winner and the other one the loser. On the other hand, the "ideal" group is the one in which this dialectic is resolved through a report to variable sum: the report "win-win", in which no one loses because everyone is committed for a collective win: one self and the others, similar ones and different ones.

As mentioned above, in order to create the conditions for the expression of group cost effectiveness, the maximum possible expression of all members of the group itself must be granted.

From The Agglutinated Group to the Grid Net Group, from the Confusing Society to the Individuals' Society

We can understand what "agglutinate" means looking at photos and footage of huge gatherings of the political period of maximalism in which individuals are organized around a mass society where the *foule* does not allow the identification of individuals, of their parts, of the specific characteristics of each one. This term refers to both the shape of the group visible from the outside, and the social representation as it is shaped in the mind and psyche of the individuals who are part of that group.

The original agglutinated "confusing" group is governed by the emotional and affective system of the maternal code where mother and child are continually confused. This is a group without distances inside and characterized by relationships, identifications and projections which tend to con-fusion, to uniqueness.

In the evolution process, the individual initiates the process of *separation-individuation* from the original nucleus by changing the passage from the confusing relationships linked to the agglutinated original group to those "grid net" based on mutual recognition and mutual accountability.

This aspect is pivotal for the establishment of subjectivity and for the identity formation. It is therefore necessary to focus on the transition from an idea of the social as agglutinated aggregation to one of reticular form/shape.

From the crowd, where everyone is almost unrecognizable, so irresponsible towards everything, to an aggregation in which individuals can recover the bonds that hold firmly people together.

---

[10] We refer to "Theory of games" (1950) introduced by John Forbes Nash

Today, thanks to new information technologies, communications arising from the individual can be multiplied into the space and through time in a complex system.

By using technology, it is possible to represent the social in the form of a network, a grid, a plot of nodes built by the individuals that are part of this aggregate.

In this process, the current communication systems help to define a representation of the Social organized around a series of relationships that, starting from any given individual, increase in space and time in a complex system.

This implies a representation of the social very different from that of the nineteenth century that Le Bon (1895), one of the founders of social psychology, discussed. Le Bon was the first psychologist to study and observe scientifically the behavior of crowds, trying to detect their peculiar characteristics and propose techniques to guide and control them. His works were read and studied by the totalitarian dictators of the twentieth century who drew inspiration from them.

Le Bon outlined a representation of the social as a mass: the so-called *foule*. He studied the psychological elements active in the mass.

In his view, the collective mind reflects the unconscious shared quality of the race. The idea of the conscious individual personality is lost. If the person acts consciously on the basis of reason, the crowd acts impulsively and in a lack of awareness on the basis of instinctual drives. The crowd, according to Le Bon, is the result of a process of de-individuation, of contamination that is a mutual imitation and suggestion that implies an irrational acceptance of mutual influence and the use of regressive negative methods.

This representation of the world clashes with the one theorized by Foulkes (1983), according to which one refers to the individuals who carry a matrix as a “grid net” capable of containing all exchanges and plots that are organized around the individual newborn and which are the very reasons of his construction. The theorized agglutinated mode is a mode among the many possible.

Norbert Elias, following the works of Le Bon and together with Foulkes, developed the sociological theory of the "society of individuals", a society made up of persons and subjects. This theory of social development proposes a kind of re-humanization of sociological categories. The dilemma "Is the individual who builds the society or is the society that builds individuals?"

Elias (1987) says:

> "what often takes place in the mind is divided as if they were two different substances or man's strata, his individuality and his social determination are no more than two different functions that human beings have in their mutual relations: they have no consistency independently [...] and every man, for better or worse, is bound to each other as a plurality, i.e. as a society "(p.8).

In other words, it is about recognizing the relational dimension of the "we" in that of the "I" and vice versa, against a sort of independence, as defined ontologically.

This contribution in addition to those on the conception of the mind as a result of the interconnection between nature and culture, between individuals, groups and communities in a relational perspective can be thought of as a graphical representation of the Moebius Ring [11] [Fig. 5]. The Moebius Ring or Moebius Strip is a surface with only one side and one edge and it has, in addition to the mathematical property of non-adjustability in the Euclidean space, the non-disjunction in resolvability.

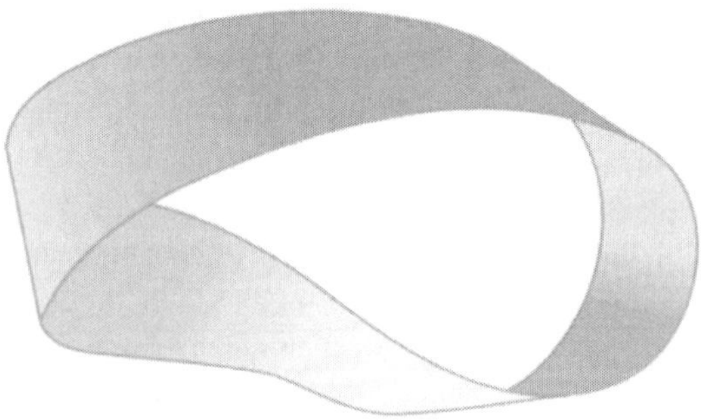

Figure 5. Moebius Ring.

The Grameen Model: The Group of Good Practice

The aspects described so far combine to determine the precise characteristics of the group that we call economic, which involves the

[11] The Moebius Ring has been discovered by two German mathematicians: A.F. Moebius and J.P. Listing in 1858.

development both of individuals and the group in a virtuous circle of resources development.

The dialectic of individual / group, basic element of this reflection, has a significant role in relation to the issue of social and economic models.

In a social context, in fact, for political, economic and cultural reasons, a situation can arise in which the group takes precedence over the individual and, vice versa, a situation in which the individual takes precedence over the group. In both cases, especially if the situation is taken to extremes, it is a relation of the type "*mors tua vita mea*" (i.e. "your death – my life"), or a *zero sum* relationship between the two parties.

We consider that the first model, the one in which the individual prevails over the group, corresponds to the culture that is expressed by the philosophy of the market economy centered on the rivalry, while the other one corresponds to the coercive socialist model in which the individual is drowned out by the group.

The model described below is, in our opinion, the representative model of what we call "good rule".

This is the microcredit conceived by Yunus, Nobel Peace Prize 2006, which, thanks to its methodology and results, is one of the best practices in this area.

The Grameen microcredit model is a tool that combines tangible and intangible assets in a virtuous plot and which consists on a social and economic "revolution" with significant consequences on the psyche of individuals in the mental representation of self, self among others, the group, the community, the social.

The reason for this assumption comes from the fact that, in its optimal achievement, microcredit aims at enhancing the ability of individuals belonging to a group; the more the individuals are able to actively take part in the group, the more the group itself give back richness to them.

The Grameen model's priority is the building of the social capital through the formation of groups and Centres[12], the development of a democratic leadership, the election of board members, since these borrowers are the owners of the bank, and various other aspects that allow maximum expression of all members of the group.

---

[12] The Grameen Bank (Head Office) is composed by different groups (every group counts 5 women), different centres (every centre counts from 6 to 8 groups) and different branch (every branch counts from 60 up to 70 centres).

Microcredit employs a working method based on the group link and it considers women as privileged users; "marginalized in work, disadvantaged economically and socially, women constitute the majority of the poor, and their bond with their children actually represent the future of the country. "(Yunus, 1998, p.89)

The Grameen device is based on a group of five people who are chosen on a trust basis as companions in adventure.

The group is a community of support and mutual exchange, whose aim is to broaden and strengthen networks of local social networks to increase the individual and collective sense of confidence. More specifically, the group works as a minimal aggregation of individuals and as the nucleus of a larger community, a community created to develop the full relational potential at its best.

In the Grameen model all group members live in the same village, know each other, often they belong to the same neighborhood but they do not come from the same family.

The group should be composed of people "like minded". Each member must have a similar point of view towards life and things, not so much to reinforce conformity, but to provide an opportunity for mirroring process with the other members of the group. At the same time, however, members will have their own specificity and diversity in the choice of the project and in its management.

With such mechanism of the group loan, the Grameen Bank establishes a relationship with each individual and enhances the system of horizontal relationships within the group. These aspects involve a natural reduction of the opportunistic mechanisms related to information asymmetry between the parties.

In addition, since the possibility of access to credit depends not only on the behavior of the single individual, but also on that of other members of the group, the peers and a virtuous and encouraging group pressure automatically trigger certain mechanisms of monitoring and support.

Yunus (1998) stated:

> “People, on their own, tend to be unpredictable and irresolute. With the support and encouragement of the group, their behaviour acquires stability and becomes consequently more reliable. The pressure, more or less discrete, exercised by the group is used to keep its members within the overall objectives of the credit program. The competition developed between groups and within the group itself encourages each individual to do his best. It is

difficult to follow the evolution of the situation of each client, but if he is part of a group, the difficulties are much lower. To appoint to the group some aspects of the control means to increase their autonomy and reduce the work of the employees. Moreover, since the group is required to approve each member's credit request, everyone feels morally involved to ensure repayment, and if someone is in trouble, the others usually, in fact, get activate to help. "(p.104).

In this way, a methodological framework is outlined in which Grameen Bank places at the heart the needs and the development of the human being rather than profit.

To better understand how Grameen Bank has planned its programs, we have followed step by step some of the rules that organize the project of the bank for the poor.

We continue to read the Grameen model keeping in mind the reference models of group analysis applied to clinics and Therapeutic Communities[13].

This methodology allowed us to identify some elements of surprising closeness that are described below:

- The Grameen groups are homogeneous groups in terms of gender and socio-economic status of the people. Initially they were constructed by mixing male and female, then limited the participation to only women. The reason for this redefinition was the desire to reduce the cultural orientations of gender predominance also in the group. As a matter of facts, such attitudes were dysfunctional compared to the entire educational and experiential project. In terms of the composition of the standard clinical group, Foulkes stresses the need of homogeneity in relation to cultural and social status as well as intelligence and age. (Di Maria & Formica, 2009)
- More people belonging to the same family cannot be part of the same group[14]. The reason for this rule is to try to avoid the conditions that favor the emergence of a subgroup, a phenomenon that is likely to cause loss of connection with the group and of it being equal and fair. In fact, being the family relationship a strong bond, this bond would

[13] We refer to various models of present communities in the United Kingdom that constitute reference models based on the planning. of patients' treatment

[14] This one and the following descriptions related to the microcredit model Grameen have been freely translated from the International Observatory on the Microfinance of the University of Bologna (www.cirig.unibo.it) and they are in the original version property of the Grameen Bank.

become, within a group of micro-credit, a discriminatory element between family members and others.

- Each group must have a *chairman* and a secretary, elected by the members of the group. This election will be held on the first meeting in which the group will be formed and then once a year. One member cannot be re-elected for a consecutive term. The reason of this rule is that everyone in the group must be put in a position to have the greatest responsibility of the group in turn. This principle is also applied to the field of Therapeutic Communities[15], with the aim of ensuring that the people, especially the borderline subjects, to whom these communities are dedicated to, can learn from experience to be responsible for the management of certain functions of the community. To put people in situations of responsibility belongs to the Grameen philosophy, because the main goal of this bank is to develop human capital, ensuring that each person is able to be part of a community that the more its members are skilled the more it is enriched.
- In certain circumstances a maximum of 10 people can get in a group. In any case, despite a centre may contain a maximum of 10 groups, the total of the components of a centre cannot exceed 70 members. This criterion/parameter is once again very significant, as attention to the proportions shows that the Grameen philosophy pursues a kind of balance that affects not only the small group, but also the set of small groups within the Center, seeking/attempting to preserve communal harmony. This is conceived in terms of position in relation to the Community and, at the same time, in terms of the identity of each individual over the group, concerning the centre and the Community. This is an optimal balance that regulates the interaction between people. In addition to this, attention is paid to the numerical / structural components of the groups, based on the belief that relationships can be built and retained only under certain conditions of group relations.

---

[15] The Henderson Hospital covers inside the English Movement of the Therapeutic Communities a very important role. It was founded by Maxwell Jones upon the base of two precedents community experiences: the one of the Mill Hill Hospital (1942-46) and the other of the Industrial Rehabilitation Unit, to the Belmont Hospital in London, beginning from the 1957. It turns, from a diagnostic point of view, to patient suffering from "serious troubles of personality."

- The chairman and the secretary have regular contact with the bank, dealing in fact also with the regularity of the loans and the refunds, and promoting participation in the meetings of the centre. It is through this regular participation, feature of the Grameen model to which someone has attributed the major cause of its uniqueness in Western countries, that a fiduciary relationship is built. Concerning the topic of absence, according to the group analysis application, "it is assumed that the group has priority over everything else for the patient, who is why the absences are strongly discouraged" (Di Maria & Formica, 2009, p. 153).
- In addition to the presence attendance, punctuality is also a crucial factor. These aspects concern obviously the leader of the group as well.
- The key issue is the discipline of the group, which is nothing more than an agreement. Before starting the micro-credit program, in fact, the future members follow a training course during which they discuss the disciplinary elements. The focus is to ensure that these are recognizable as necessary and shared by all the participants. These are not imposed rules, but shared, in agreement with everyone through the empowerment of all.
- Each group member should have a complete and adequate knowledge of the rules, of the group regulations and their individual responsibilities. The knowledge of the rules, and their acceptance and internalization by each member of the group simultaneously, creates a single indivisible body. Because the rules are the same for all members, nobody has interest in having privileges and nobody fears punishment. The rules assume/take on the role of what Rousseau (1789) called "General Will". The knowledge and the acceptance of the rules thus give rise to a moral body, where everyone talks to everyone, without ever losing more than what they earn. In fact, increasing the force to maintain what they already have. The violation of individual responsibility can only, in this context, depend on the non-acceptance of the rules, then a primal attitude of the individual who, from the beginning chooses, not to join the group.
- If a member demonstrates to work against the discipline of the group (for example, to be absent for many times, to have no interest in paying the money back) the others may suggest expulsion after a shared discussion. Here, a clear parallel to the Therapeutic

Communities arises: if someone violates the rules, in fact, it is the community itself to decide for or against the exclusion of the member.

- If a member leaves the group for personal reasons, can re-enter later, but only after three months and after repeating the initial training. Once again, this policy demonstrates a special attention both to the individual, who is not punished but engaged again as if he was a new member, and towards the group that cannot be changed or abandoned without consequences for individuals who are part of it. The group-orientation, in this regard, distinguishes the groups as open, closed and semi-open precisely in terms of the possibility to allow / not allow the entry / the exit of a member. Such events modify the identity of the group and bring about particularly delicate situations, since they alter the group-analytical setting and the identity of the group itself.
- The *Centre manager*, during the meeting, registers the presence of all members of the group, the refund of regular savings and loans and the whole discipline of the centre. As the responsible of the centre, the group leader as well is required to administer and to interpret. This person must have a leadership role and it is recommended that he keeps a register of attendance and payment of the sessions.
- If, within three months, the centre manager does not attend half or more of the meetings, his place will be considered vacant; in that case a new Centre manager must be elected. As mentioned earlier, the conductor as well has the obligation to respect and embrace the rules of the group involved in the clinic as in the Grameen model. This denotes the fact that the group is always the centre of attention and it is the respect of the group which establishes the rules: the social bond.

CONCLUSION

This reflection has led us to identify the solution that Yunus proposes: a relationship between individuals and group type "win-win". In fact, the individual gives to the group his resources which, circulating in a trade network, reach other individuals who, in turn, offer and receive group resources that the group has drawn up, thus making the final solution a benefit to all.

The Grameen group has cost effectiveness, according the perspective that we have described above, because it increases the resources of both parties: the individual and the group.

The model proposed by Yunus is suspended between vertical and horizontal elements, and it is, among the various experiences of microcredit existing in the world, certainly the most important and the one with the best results.

The several micro-credit initiatives, where the vertical element prevails, lead to vertical reciprocity, recalling the relationship which is basically authoritarian/charitable (e.g. micro-credit with a guarantor). At the same time, there are others initiatives characterized by a horizontal reciprocity. Obviously, if the micro-credit initiative is not bound by the conductive part of the bank, but it focuses on the subjects that make up the group, the probability of a horizontal reciprocity is greater.

Practical experiences are situated in different parts of the continuum between authoritarian and horizontal reciprocity, and a lot depends on the context in which these experiences are developed.

To support individual-group dialectic of win-win type/kind means to provide the individual, the citizen the opportunity to contribute to the creation of community wealth that, in turn, gives wealth back to the citizen.

The group in which relational goods circulate is not necessarily the best group: it has cost effectiveness if it allows people to find more solutions to their problems, to increase the spectrum of possibilities and if it ensures consistency between its *raison d'être* and its functioning.

Figuratively speaking, the economic group could be described as a choir in which each component has to find a harmony with each other, in order to offer his voice in a collective sound "space" that does not exclude the possibility of solo voices.

In other words, Justice from the ethical point of view is harmony in terms of the participation of all voices

References

Acts of the conference *The economy of the group. Relational Goods in society, mind and brain.* Venice, 2002.

Brunori, L. (2008). *Money for peace. Disrespect today, conflict tomorrow.* Center for post conflict- Nottingham University- U.K., pp.79-90.

Brunori, L. (2003). Relational Goods in Society, Mind and Brain: Between Neurons and Happiness. *Group Analysis Vol.16* n.4, pp. 515-525.

Brunori, L., & Bleve, C. (2009). *La finanza dei poveri*. Micromega. Roma: Gruppo Editoriale L'Espresso, 3/09.

Brunori, L., & Raggi, C. (2007). *Le comunità terapeutiche*. Bologna: Il Mulino.

Di Maria, F., & Lo Verso, G. (1995). *La Psicodinamica dei Gruppi: teorie e tecniche*. Milano: Raffaello Cortina Editore.

Elias, N. (1987). Die Gesellschaft der Individuen. Frankfurt: Suhrkamp. *Trad it. La società degli individui.* (1990). Saggi. Bologna: Il Mulino.

Fasolo, F. (1990). Fattori terapeutici in psicoterapia di gruppo. In G. Di Marco (Ed.) *I fattori di cambiamento in terapia*. (pp. 39-46). Chieti: Metis Editrice.

Foulkes, S. H. (1983). *Introduction to Group-Analytic Psychotherapy: Studies in the Social Integration of Individuals and Groups*. London: Maresfield Reprints.

Foulkes, S. H. (1968). On interpretation in group analysis. *International J. Group Psychotherapy*, 18, pp. 432-434.

Foulkes, S. H. (1975). A Short Outline of the Therapeutic Processes in Group-Analytic Psychotherapy. *Group Analysis*, 2; vol. 8, pp. 60 -63.

Foulkes, S. H., & Anthony, E. J.(1998). *L'approccio psicoanalitico alla psicoterapia di gruppo*. Roma: Edizioni Universitarie Romane.

Fukuyama, F. (1995). *Trust*. London: Penguin Books.

Heinzel, R., Breyer, F. & Klein, T. (2000). *Outpatient Psychoanalytic Individual and Group Psychotherapy in a Nationwide Catamnestic Study in Germany*. Group Analysis 33(3), pp. 353-372.

Le Bon, G. (1895) Psychologie des foules. Paris: PUF. Trad it. *Psicologia delle folle. Milano:TEA Editore*, 2004.

MacKenzie, K. R. (1995). *Effective use of group therapy in managed care*. Washington: American Psychiatric Press.

Nash, J.F. (1950). Equilibrium points in n-person games, *Proceedings of the National Academy of the USA*.

Phillipson, N. (2010). Adam Smith. *An Enlightened life*. London: Allen Lane.

Pines, M. (1978). The Contributions of S.H. Foulkes to Group Analytic Psychotherapy. In Wolberg, Aronson, Wolberg (Eds) *Group Therapy: An Overview*. New York: Stratton Intercontinental Medical Book Corporation.

Pines, M. (1981). The Frame of Reference of Group Psychotherapy. *International Journal of Group Psychotherapy,* Vol. 31, No. 3, pp. 275-85.

Pines, M. (1968). Group Analysis. In G. Gazda (Ed.). *Basic Approaches to Group Psychotherapy and Group Counselling.* Illinois: Charles C. Thomas.

Polanyi, K. (1974).*La grande trasformazione*. Torino:Einaudi.

Rousseau, J.J. (1979) *Article Six of the Déclaration des droits de l'Homme et du citoyens.*

Sen, A. K. (1985). *Commodities and Capabilities*. Amsterdam: North-Holland.

Spaltro, E., (1970). *Gruppi e cambiamento.* Milano: Etas Kompass.

Stiglitz J. (1990). Peer Monitoring and Credit Markets. *World bank Economic Review,* Vol .4 (3).

Stiglitz, J.E. (2002). *La globalizzazione e i suoi oppositori*. Torino: Einaudi.

Tschuschke, V., & Mackenzie, K. R. (1989) Empirical analysis of group development: a methodological report. *Small Group Behaviour*, 20, pp. 419-427.

Tschuschke,V. & Anbeh, T. (2000) Early Treatment Effect of Long-Term Outpatient Group Therapies. First Preliminary Result. *Group Analysis, Vol. 33,* 3, pp. 397-411.

Ulhaner , C. J. (1989). Relational Goods and Participation: Incorporating Sociability into a Theory of Rational Action. *Public Choice Journal*, Vol.62, pp. 253-285.

Yunus, M. (1997). *Vers un monde sans pauvreté.* Paris: Éditions Jean-Claude Lattès.

Yunus, M. (2008). *Creating a World without Poverty: Social Business and the Future of Capitalism.* Ney York: Public Affairs.

Zamagni, S. (2006). *L'economia come se la persona contasse: verso una teoria economica relazionale*. Working Paper n.32, Bologna.

In: The Other Side of the Coin
Editors: L. Brunori and M. Pines
ISBN: 978-1-62618-726-9

Chapter 3

SOCIAL BRAIN AND SOCIAL GROUP: HOW MIRRORING CONNECTS PEOPLE

Malcolm Pines*
Institute of Group Analysis, London

ABSTRACT

A theoretically infinite range of exchanges may take place within the group. This chapter will examine mirroring as one type of exchange group. It will be shown that mirroring, besides being a tool for communication between individuals, also corresponds to the basic function of developing knowledge and connection between people. Recent findings in the field of the neurosciences have shown the presence of 'mirror neurons' in the neural system of primates and humans. These neurons make possible exchanges between people, the development of the psyche and the inter-subjective processes that are a basic condition for knowledge acquisition from others, and for development of relational life.

INTRODUCTION

Human beings are enabled to create and live in complex societies as through language and gestures we are able to convey and receive meaningful

* Correspondence regarding this chapter may be addressed to Malcolm Pines Email: *malcpines@btinternet.com;*

information. Isolation from society, by exile, hazards of becoming lost threaten to dehumanize the person. Becoming sane members of societies is built upon chains of dependency and interdependency. Adam Smith wrote that Society is a Mirror for the person, that with ought that mirror the person will never come to know herself. Visual mirroring and acoustic mirroring [resonance] connect people in social networks. Persons are formed as nodes in these networks.

Microcredit and Group Analysis

Smith's (1759; 1776) emphasis on sympathy and mirroring brings economics close to group analysis, where interpersonal relations, mirroring and resonance, are intrinsic to the enterprise translation which Foulkes[1] had emphasized from the start. We are all incomplete persons who seek our wholeness, our validation from the gaze, gestures and verbal responses of others. Economic theory emphasizes factors such as social capital the source of benefit for a community which may be rich or scanty, available to all to benefit from.

Another aspect of economic theory is the distinction between positional and relational goods. The latter are goods which can be achieved when persons enter unto relations which benefit them: trust, friendship, cooperation, mutual support and relational goods which instead of being used up increase through the experience of working together. The contrast is with hierarchical goods; the hierarchy, the ladder of promotion to the top, the pyramid or greasy pole, where success is achieved though competition, success or failure; self-satisfaction, jealously and envy are intrinsic.

A striking example of the economic value of relational goods is the microcredit bank, which started as the Grameen Bank in Bangladesh where Muhammad Yunus the Professor of Economics at Dhaka found that peasants were locked in a cycle of poverty and debt as they had no economic credit worth and were in the clutches of loan sharks who penalized them with very high interest rates. Yunus set up his own bank and loaned small amounts sufficient to help peasants to break free of the cycle of poverty by purchasing seeds for crops, simply machines for weaving and other simple necessities.

---

[1] Siegfried Heinrich Foulkes (1898–1976) was the founder of Group Analysis, a specific form of group therapy, and the Group Analytic Society, London, which has an international membership in many countries.

Importantly the loan is made not to an individual, it is to a group. The forces of group dynamics are utilized.

The microcredit movement is now worldwide and has benefited very many persons.

Now for neuroscience. The University of Parma is a close neighbor of the University of Bologna. Here is a leading school of neuroscience lead by Giacomo Rizzolatti (1992). They were the first to isolate and to identify the mirror neurons, first identified in monkeys in the part of the brain equivalent to Brocas area, the main speech area. These multivalent neurons are activated when the animal makes a meaningful gesture such as grasping or tearing. The same neuron fires when another animal, in this case a man, performs the same movement. Thus it seems that the mirror neuron mechanism, which is auditory as well as visual, is the neurological substrate for recognizing the intent of the other: the path of inter-subjectivity, of crossing the solipsistic gap, of getting beyond the isolation of each person in his/her skull. Notable is the recent finding that autistic children are significantly deficient in mirror neurons.

Neuroscience now has the means to register the brain areas activated in to sympathy, empathy, trust and mistrust. The outcome of these relevant studies of the relational sciences, economics, neuroscience, is the institution of a new doctorate of the University of Bologna in relational sciences.

THE SOCIAL BRAIN

"What is the social brain?"

We are social animals embedded in networks of relationships without which we cannot survive. Human beings have the greatest capacity of all animals to create and control their environment, their portion of nature. Humans are cultured animals who have the brain capacity to develop cultural communities.

Writing about the evolutionary origins of our social brain, Merlin Donald (1991), an influential researcher and writer states:

> "Human beings are cultural entities. We share mind. We construct cognitive collectivities called symbolic cultures. Raised in isolation from such collectivities we have quite limited non-symbolic minds. Culturally isolated human beings are not much different from their large brained anthropoid relatives. However, embedded in the cultural network from birth,

human beings become something unique in the biological world; symbolizing intellects bonded to a community of minds." (p. 215)

The book "*Origins of the Modern Mind*" was and still is a great stimulus of our thinking of how our human social brain emerges from primates. Donald insists that culture is fundamentally important in forming the social brain and mind. Our human mind evolved through a series of three major adaptations at each of which there emerged new representational systems, leading to our symbolic capacities.

The progression is: from primates by developing gestural, linguistic and thought structures. In this first stage of "mimes" gestural communication, cooperation and social coordination of actions were central to species' survival strategies. Mimetic cultures enable individuals to create group structures with social roles and group norms. Knowledge can be transmitted, acknowledged and shared. Social brain, distributed knowledge.

The second transmission is from mimetic to mythic cultures. These pass on collective knowledge about survival through a vast heritage; oral lore, totemic art, mimetic song, dance and ritual. Language is in the form of narrative; symbolic art appears.

Humans now coin synthesised symbolic art and symbolic language. Writing emerges, therefore memory can now be held in "external storage systems"; knowledge can be retrieved, critically examined, leading to theoretic culture.

As humans evolve through these stages, brain structures and capacities appear, not increase in brain mass but in brain capacities; encephalisation, network capacities. Biology and technology now are a single evolutionary continuum.

In recent writing Merlin Donald states: "[..] distributed knowledge, distributed networks engaging other minds, interlinking minds, using technology. Today's world wide web is the latest of these stages, emerging from smaller, slower mechanism. The human mind becomes more powerful by its connection to community networks." (ibid.)

Donald does not refer to Norbert Elias' studies of networks of dependency but expresses similar ideas in writing that it is difficult for us to accept the degree of our dependency, our "grand illusion of individuality" is defined by our fixed places in a particular community network. We gain intellectual status when we are wedded to a community of mind.

Dunbar's (1998) work is to link brain size and complexity to the ability to live in complex large groups. He uses the volume of the neo-cortex as the measure of brain size because this accounts for most of the brain expansion in primates. Measure of social complexity correlates with relative neo-cortical volume. The volume of neo-cortex imposes a limit on the number of relationships that individual primates can sustain in their mental model of their social world[2]. Dunbar asserts that the human social group and clique size from neo-cortical volumes are: 150 for social group size, 12 for a more intimate clique size. Dunbar cites as evidence for the 150-group size: average village size in Domseday Book; the common size of self-sustainable military groups such as a company. Within these groups of 150 there are hierarchical structures of friendship. Five intimates for support, 15 for close friendships and sympathy, 50 is the next larger group size, then 150 as the outer limit of relationships. The microcredit group is 5, thus giving support.

What now can be added is the knowledge of the striking differences between the sexes in social mechanisms and brain units involved. Female sociality is more affiliative, is related closely to neo-cortical volumes whereas male sociality is more competitive and combative, more closely related to sub-cortical units, the limbic system and hypothalamus. This suggests that the male and female brains have responded to different kinds of social pressures. Females to social integration, males to male-to-male competitiveness and fighting. As the level of competition between males increases, the level of cortical control is reduced (Dunbar, 2007).

Byrne and Whiten (1988) termed their model of the unusual complexity of the primate social world where tactical deception and coalition formations feature as the *"Machiavellian Intelligence Hypothesis"*; later this was renamed the *"Social Brain Hypothesis"* so as to remove it from imputations of political machination.

Later Dunbar suggests that story telling and religion are consequences of the capacities for social cognition: they require us to be able to imagine virtual worlds that have no immediate experiential context and requires us that those who we ask to share this imaginary world can genuinely follow us on this journey, this religious journey. In story telling we have to imagine a fictional world. The ability to work in a fictional world is an especially demanding cognition which is only possible to animals such as the great apes and humans who have developed large neo-cortices. The same applies to sharing the ability to imagine the existence of another universe.

---

[2] Here we should acknowledge De Mare's writings on human group size, which he derived from the size of the ancient Icelandic parliaments.

Cozolino (2006) calls the interpersonal space "the social synapse" that has to be bridged and by which we are linked to society, to families, to collectivities. The sensory experience of social communication, deeply woven into who we are, helps regulate physiological and emotional equilibrium. The social environment affects the neuronal and hormonal signals that govern our body and behaviour and in turn create changes in the social brain that affect our neural and hormonal processes. The UCLA Loneliness Scale gives us a measure of a person's sense of interconnectedness or isolation. Research with young and older adults has shown that those who were lonelier had larger numbers of objective stresses in their lives. The consequences of their "self-protective" behaviour over time led to interpersonal and social problems significantly more than those reported who themselves as connected and contented. The chronic heightened stresses can lead to various types of physiological damage shown by heightened cortisol levels.

Cozolino (2006) writes: "The brain is an organ of adaptation that builds its structures through interaction with others. There are no single brains, the arguments equally apply to the concept of a social mind". (p. 447)

Experience leaves traces that modify what went before. The connections among neurons are permanently modified by experience, thus the brain must be thought of as a highly dynamic organ in permanent relation with the environment as well as with the psychic facts of the subject or his acts. The brain can no longer be seen as a fixed organ, determined and determining once and for all. Plasticity shows that the neuronal network remains open to change, to contingency, that it can be modified by events and the potentiality of experience which can always alter what has come before. Plasticity shows how the brain changes through the stages of life and most importantly how the effects of psychotherapy can stimulate neuronal changes giving us the opportunity, a way out from repetition or fixed patterns: a biology of freedom.

Mirror Neurons

These were discovered at the beginning of the 1990s and show how recognition of the actions of others, and even of their intentions, depends first of all on our motor repertoire. From elementary acts such as grasping to the more sophisticated that require particular skills such as playing a sonata on a pianoforte or executing complicated dance steps, mirror neurons allow our brain to match the movements we observe to the movements we ourselves perform, and so to appreciate their meaning. Without a mirror mechanism we would still have our sensory representations, a "pictorial" depiction of the behavior of others, but we would not know what they were really doing.

It would seem therefore that the mirror neurons system is indispensable to that sharing of experience which is at the root of our capacity to act as individuals and as members of a society. Forms of imitation, both simple and complex, of learning, of verbal and gestural communication, presuppose the activation of specific mirror circuits. Our capacity to appreciate the emotional reactions of others is correlated to a particular group of brain areas that are characterized by mirror properties. Emotions, like actions, are immediately shared; the perception of pain or grief or of disgust experienced by others, activates the same areas of the cerebral cortex that are involved when we ourselves experience these emotions.

This shows how strong and deeply rooted is the bond that ties us to others, or in other words, "How bizarre it would be to conceive of an I without an us" (Rizzolatti & Sinigaglia, 2008, pp. xii–xiii).

These mirror neurons were first identified in monkeys but have now been also identified in humans. Mirror neurons allow the brain to match movements we observe to the movements we ourselves can perform and so to appreciate their meaning without a need for reasoning. As written above they are indispensable for that sharing of experience which is at the root of our capacity to act as individuals but also as members of society. The presence of this brain mechanism and capacity provides us with the data to support the theories of George Herbert Mead (1930).

Mead described what he saw as "the language of gestures" in animals, that seemed to understand and respond to the intentions of another and he extends this to humans. We understand the meaning of the language and the meaning of the gestures of another human being because we ourselves can use that language and make those same gestures. It is interesting that the research with monkey evolved from seeing the neuronal stimulation when the monkey either itself grasped an object or saw another animal or person grasping the same object.

We humans speak about understanding and grasping meanings. To understand means to stand under, that is to put oneself physically and mentally into the place of the other and grasp refers to the mental act of understanding a meaning. So mirror neurons enable us to understand the meaning of motor events, of actions performed by others and how to immediately recognize a specific type of action and differentiate it from another. We use the information to respond appropriately to the movements made by another. Thus we perceive the meaning of "motor events" and interpret them in terms of an intentional act. We build up in our brains a vocabulary of acts so that when we see someone replicating this action our motor system goes into *resonance mode* by which we recognize the intentional aspects of the movements and understand the type of action, which then determines our response. Looking at it from the point of view of evolution this shows how built in to our brain activated motor system is the knowledge how to defend ourselves by parrying the movements of the other. This is beautifully exemplified by Japanese martial arts such as Akaido where the learner is taught how to anticipate and to parry the act of the other.

Cozolino (2006) describes how in learning Akaido he had a confrontation with an Akaido master. He stepped towards the master and in a very short time without having made physical contact with him he found himself thrown to the ground:

> "..my teacher was a master at activating and manipulating balance, reflexes, neuro-systems and resonance behaviors. He was playing my body like a familiar instrument and I understood his calm in the face of attack; I was easy prey. It was a humbling lesson on both my lack of skill as an Akaido-ist and of the power of these automatic and unconscious resonance reactions." (p. 272)

When I was learning Tai Chi I saw the same phenomenon, that is the students stepping towards the master to engage with him and finding themselves repelled without any apparent movement on the part of the master. Merleau-Ponty (1962) wrote: "The sense of gesture is not given, but understood, that is recaptured by an act on the spectator's part. There is a reciprocity of my intentions discernible in others. It is as if the other person's intentions inhabited my body and mine his."(p. 185).

There is a "shared space of action" within which each act and chain of acts are immediately registered and understood.

Bridging the Solipsistic Gulf

Humans have learnt how to use chemical mechanisms (oxytocin, vasopressin, endorphins) to manipulated their own and each other's behavior in order to build the channels of communication that are required to overcome the "solipsistic gulf" in forming societies. Music, dancing and sports provide the archetypal techniques. Neurons are designed by biological evolution to work in pairs, families, tribes and by cultural evolution from this biological base into cities, nations and empires. There are biological properties by which brains join together in social co-operation. Intentionality is central to Freeman's thesis (1995), in his usage intentionality means the process of the brain in action having properties of unity, wholeness and intent:

- an *intentional structure* is a living brain having the capacity to actualize these properties by purposive behavior.
- *unity* refers to a state of integration by which a self-distinguishes itself from non-self. This property attaches to bacteria, neurons, brains, and the immune systems of multi-cellular animals.
- *wholeness* refers to a bounded process by which through stages a self-actualizes its mature form, ultimately to die, holding for plants, animals, brains and healing bodies.
- *intent* refers to a relationship in which the self modifies itself into conformant with aspects of non-self.

Intentionality is a central concept for Freeman. He asserts that the brain substance, the *neuropil* which consists of nerve cells, axons, dendrites and the surrounding glia, demonstrate this intentionality and the search for communicating between one brain and another is shown by this "stretching forth". Piaget shows that children learn about the world using their bodies to explore it by "stretching forth". Merleau-Ponty (1945) shows that human mental activities shape themselves by adapting bodily movements towards biological goals in everyday tasks: "to perceive is to render oneself present to something through the body". Merleau-Ponty describes the *intentional arc,* which constitutes the effort to achieve maximum grip. It self-adapts to an object and learns about it by shaping the body and by re-shaping or re-positioning the object, e.g. manipulating a new tool. We are moved to action by disequilibrium between the self and the world. Freeman does not refer to Paul Schilder and his concept of body image where Schilder (1935) shows that the body image is constantly changing in relation to experiences in the world, particularly by emotional and physical contact with other bodies.

Freeman (2001) writes: each of us is a source of meaning, a well-spring for the flow of fresh constructions within our brains and bodies, sheltered by the privacy of isolation. Our intentional actions continually flow into the world, changing the world and the relation of our bodies to it. This dynamic system is the self in each of us. It is the agency of charge, not our awareness, which is constantly trying to catch up with what we do. We perceive the world from inside our boundaries as we gauge it and then change ourselves by assimilation.

FRIDAY'S FOOTPRINTS

Leslie Brother (1997) is a psychiatrist, neuro-scientist and psychoanalyst. She makes the strongest case for the social brain and possibly was the first to use that term. She uses Defoe's fictional character Robinson Crusoe, who lived in isolation for 25 years until he saw the footprints of another human being which led him to the native whom he gave the name Friday, because that was the day upon which he discovered him. Brother uses Robinson Crusoe as a metaphor for the belief in the isolated human mind that was current in the 18th century biology. Brothers emphasizes that culture arises from a network of meanings from the interactivity of human brains. This network forms the living content of the mind so the mind is communal is very nature. Brains work jointly to create culture, human conversations hold the key to the mind. Primate brains evolved to send and receive facial gestures, which eventually led to discourse. The interchange of expressions is a jointly created performance whose nature is essentially public. The concept of the person always belong to a network of persons.

THE "SOCIAL ORDER"

The social order is intrinsically moral for it is made up of "*oughts and shoulds*", good and evil, pride and shame, villains and heroes. When we hear words we experience not only the meaning of the word but that it indicates the presence of a person who has both subjectivity and location in the social order. This is what was already discovered in the vocalization of baboons, that when a baboon hears a vocalization it knows which family that one belongs to, position in the social order in the hierarchy. A characteristic of autism is that autistic children do not attend to the social situation, therefore do not receive social information and are not drawn to the sights and sounds of others. Understanding utterances, attributing them to persons are fundamentally intertwined. This is what autistic persons do not register as they avoid looking at facial gestures and do not read from the eyes of others. Peter Hobson (1993) from the Tavistock believes that autistic children lack what is necessary for reciprocal and emotionally charged relationship with others.

SOCIAL NEURONS

Single neurons have been identified in brain areas traditionally associated with emotions and form a brain mechanism that has evolved to respond to significant gestures and expressions and form what can be called a "social module". The primate brain evolved a specialized system for producing mutually regulated behavior in complex social environments. The gestures of others are included in brain areas that index it by automatically linking it to the appropriate response. Thus an innate "social alphabet" is built up. This leads to knowledge of what the other means by immediately linking it inwardly with a response. So it seems that through evolution brains evolved in a highly social environment, therefore beyond primates humans added the conceptual level to perception of a fellow human being's mind developed that through its tie to the social order (instead of snarls and grimaces the mind registers "*shoulds and oughts*". I suggest that we can link this development to Foulkes' emphasis on "norms", the social shoulds and oughts, the dynamic that moves groups towards the social norms even though each person might represent a deviation from the norm.

PSYCHOGENESIS AND SOCIOGENESIS

A major contribution of Norbert Elias (1982) to the issues of how culture moulds the brain is this thesis: the constant evolution of society leads to changes in the personality of persons as they adapt to the evolving environment. Hence society, social processes, both frame and enter into its members from the start of life. Attitudes towards pregnancy, sexuality, maternity; child-rearing, education, gender roles, family life; rituals marking the person's move from being a child to adolescence and adulthood. Each is immersed in the culture of the community.

Elias traced the descent of manners using as his source material the books of etiquette used to instruct young noblemen on how to behave in courtly society, laying down behaviors to be followed and behaviors to be avoided: how to control the body, its appetites and excretions, how to find one's place in the social hierarchy of the court. Elias showed the development of courtly life, of what was expected, allowed, or disallowed. The sense of privacy develops as living quarter arrangements allow private spaces; thresholds for what is allowed are disallowed are gradually raised with the growth of civility; civility imposes ways of behavior: how to keep the peace, to recognize, respect, the lives of others. What in the past was allowed is now disallowed as the barrier of shame rises so that one does not indulge in the cruel practices towards other humans and towards animals; jeering at mentally disturbed people or criminals is modified and channeled via the media rather than personally going to the asylum or to the prison.

How neuroscience can be applied to these social processes can be seen through the concept of neuroplasticity. This concept names the realization that our brains are constantly engaged in dynamic processes throughout the whole of the lifespan. Norman Doidge (2007) writes that not only does the brain shape culture, culture shapes the brain. Culture is not just produced by the brain; it is also by definition a series of activities that shape the mind. The definition of culture in the Oxford English Dictionary is, "The cultivating or development [..] of the mind, faculties, manners, [..] improvement or refinement by education and training, the training development and refinement of the mind taste and manners."

This is precisely what Elias shows us and which can now be translated into the concept of the culturally modified brain. Changes in culture make for changes in the brain. We all have what might be called a culturally modified brain. The evolution of cultures, the evolution of societies is through the transmission of knowledge. This non-genetic transmission has been entitled, "Memes, culturally transmitted knowledge". The powers of culture in determining our very basic functions such as perception has been demonstrated by experiments into how persons from the individualized western cultures and from the more inter-related eastern cultures perceive situations.

In his important book *"Brain and Culture. Neurobiology, Ideology and Social Changes"* psychiatrist and psychoanalyst Bruce Wexler (2006) writes that:

> "Human beings alter the environment that shapes their brains to a degree without precedent among animals. These human alterations in the shared social environment include physical structures, laws and other codes of behaviour, food and clothes, spoken and written language, and music and other arts. In recent decades, children in Euro-American societies have been

> raised in an almost entirely human created environment. It is this ability to shape the environment that in turn shapes our brains and has allowed human adaptability and capability to develop at a much faster rate than is possible through alteration of the genetic code itself. This transgenerational shaping of the brain function through culture also means that processes that govern the evolution of societies and cultures have a great influence on how our individual brains and minds work." (p. 136)

Wexler reviews animal studies and comes to the conclusion that these studies provide evidence, then, that our brains (and minds) develop concrete perceptual structures, capabilities, and sensitivities based on common reaches of the environment in which we are reared, and then are more able and more likely to see those features in a sensory mix of new environments we encounter. Or conversely, we have a limited ability to see even common features of new environment if those features were absent from our rearing environment.

An important point that Wexler emphasises that:

> "Through instrumental parenting, adults create the physical world experienced and acted in by children, and interactively intervene in the object-activities of children. In these interventions adults provide frontal lobe functions of which the child is not yet capable (e.g. memory, planning, organisation and strategy) and that enable the earlier maturing sensory, motor, and association areas of the brain to develop as components of more complex functional systems. The frontal lobes, which are so much larger in humans than in other primates, then develop under the influence of activity from the externally structured, earlier maturing, cortical regions as well as from continuing social interactions. Language, itself a social and cultural development of brain capability, has radically increased the power of adults to increase the development of the brain in children." (ibid.).

The psychoanalyst Hans Loewald (1975) has made the same point in psychoanalytic terms: adults and children live in a shared psychosocial field in which the adult is at the more developed and more structured pole and the child at the less structured pole. In the course of development, also in the course of psychotherapy, these positions alter as the child, or the patient, acquire capacities that previously were found only in the adult. This is a move towards autonomy for the child and a greater capacity for self-analysis in the patient.

Finally, it is possible to identify some parallels between neurobiology and group analysis:

1) the brain is a social organ.
2) big Groups require big brains to follow the complexity of relationships.
3) vital learning takes place during interdependency.(Neoteny).
4) relationships provide the brain's environment.
5) eye to eye contact contributes vitally to attachment.
6) neural networks are formed by the interaction of organism and environment.
7) the brain is a social organ dedicated to receiving, processing and communicating messages across the "social synapse".
8) the right brain develops first; organizes and stores many social and emotional experiences: shared unconscious dialogues. Medial prefrontal cortex (OMPFC) activated in scaffolding. Left brain is biased to positive emotions, the right to negative.
9) experience-dependent phenomena. The growth of the brain is activated through emotional availability and reciprocal interactions.

THE MIRROR NEURON AS THE BASIS FOR COOPERATION AND TRUST

The biologist Patrick Bateson (1998) writing on the biological evolution of cooperation and trust, suggests that signals that predict what one individual is about to do and mechanisms for responding appropriately, would have become mutually beneficial, maintaining and enhancing coherence of highly functional cooperative behavior. Maintaining social systems that promote quick interpretation of the actions of familiar individuals would have become important. Increasing sensitiveness and self-awareness become advantageous in developing cooperation.

Whether or not a group survives depends upon the emission and reception of signals which foster cooperation; cooperation improves the adaptive features of a particular group. Successful cooperation is the basis for the development of trust.

Cooperation is essential for the functioning and survival in the animal kingdom. At the level of primates, there has evolved a brain necessary for self-recognition. It seems to me likely that the existence of the mirror neuron, which allows recognition of the actions of another member of the same species, may be the neurological basis for mirror self-recognition. It should be interesting to know whether the mirror neuron is activated by seeing oneself in a mirror. However, we know that the mirroring that contributes so importantly to developing a sense of oneself comes from the action of others, their empathy, everyday mind-reading, (Ciaramicoli, 2000), sensitive responsiveness, that promotes a sense of togetherness, at-oneness, which is the basis of relational inter-subjectivity. As Bakhtin (1993) and other psychologists and philosophers have emphasized, human self-awareness develops on the basis of *alterity*; we gain ourselves through relations with others and the other always resides deeply, unconsciously, in the depths of ourselves.

It is through the mirroring and resonance in group-analytic groups that the otherness in ourselves can enter consciousness, which is the essential condition for integration of the self, beginning the slow process of exchange, for Self-Development through Subjective Interaction (Brown, 2000). As Brown has shown us, there are 3 stages in the process of self-development in group analysis: fuller *discovery* of I in the world, which allows us to *discern* the difference between old internal object relations and new ones, and in the step towards maturity to *learn* to attune ourselves to *other people's experience as well as our own.*

It is suggested that the mirror neuron system stores and encodes unconscious non-reflective behavior patterns, that patterns of responses that are called *procedural memory,* the unconscious memory of how things are done, as opposed to *semantic memory*, which is a conscious verbal recall.

Lastly, I shall briefly discuss that form of acoustic mirroring that we call resonance. You will recall that Foulkes described resonance as the individual responses that group members make to shared events, each responding at their own level of attunement to the predominant affect in the group. We study the individual responses that are made to a shared event. I believe that acoustic neurons that respond to sound rather than to sight have also been identified and form the neurological structure that allows for response to sounds and of course, eventually, to words.

On the psychodynamic level, we can observe responses of mirroring and resonance, and non-mirroring and non-resonance in participants in small groups. Non-resonance stands out in the group as an inability to take part in exchange and dialogue. This can be observed in borderline patients, psychosomatic patients, the emotionally illiterate person, for whom the language of emotions is alien. It is fascinating to witness changes that can occur in the growth of the capacity to listen and to be listened to with understanding, development of a language that can grasp recurrent, subtle states of feelings, to see, to hear such a person begin to tune to the emotional life of others. In the analytic group non-resonance can progress to resonance, non-mirroring to mirroring in a way beyond what is possible in dyadic therapy. We can see the person re-entering, or perhaps entering for the first time, into an inter-subjective world.

Russell Mears (2000) has described non-resonance as a process that follows when the child has not developed a sense of inner value. This arises from a failure of matching between inner feelings and outer responses. When proto-conversations and the other processes of state sharing, state attunement, sensitive responsiveness, sensitive contingency and agency have been "good enough", a sense of inner value becomes part of the core self.

There is an inner conversation between asking and responding parts of the self, which maintain the sense of a good fit with the world. "The pleasure which generates a sense of value comes from a harmony, or resonance, between inner states and the outer world. This kind of relatedness, which is more than mere congruence, is essential to satisfactory development". (2000, p.68).

Surely this is the basis of psychotherapy, the sense of value that develops when a person feels understood and thereby feels valued. There is a feeling of well-being which arises when responses of the other resonate with what is sensed as being the most personal of one's experience. This is the essence of progress in group analysis, the presence of other-resonating persons whose inner processes are made both visible and audible through mirroring and resonance.

CONCLUSION

Now we can celebrate our understanding of the three vectors that reveal to us the therapeutic power of the group: neuro-dynamics, psychodynamics, economic theory. The school of Rizzolatti, the school of Foulkes, the school of Adam Smith, Zamagni, Gui, the historians and philosophers of economics.

Through the convergence of these sciences, our wealth of knowledge, our intellectual and social capital is increasing. It is said of social capital that *to consume it is to produce it,* that social capital does not wear out with use, rather with disuse, that like trust it grows, rather than diminishes with consumption. This was the aim of this chapter, to consume new knowledge and thereby add to it.

REFERENCES

Bateson, P. (1998). *The Biological Evolution of Cooperation and Trust*. In D. Gambetta (Ed) *Trust. Making and breaking cooperative relations*. Oxford: Blackwell.

Bion, W. R. (1992). *Cogitations*. London: Karnac Books.

Bronk, R. (1998). *Progress and the Invisible Hand. The Philosophy of Economics and Human Advance*. London: Little Brown.

Brothers, L. (1997). *Friday's Footprints. How society shapes the human mind*. Oxford: Oxford University Press.

Brown, D. (2000). *The Psyche and the Social World. Developments in Group Analytic Theory*. London: Jessica Kingsley Publications.

Brown, D. (2000). *Self-development through subjective interaction: a fresh look at ego training in action*. In D. Brown, & L. Zinkin, (Eds) *The Psyche and the Social World. Developments in Group Analytic Theory*. London: Jessica Kingsley Publications.

Ciaramicoli A. (2000). *The Power of Empathy*. London: J. Piatkus.

Cozolino, L. (2006). *The Neuroscience of Human Relationships*. New York: W.W. Norton & Co.

Donald, M. (1991). *Origins of Modern Mind. Three Stages in the Evolution of Culture and cognition*. Cambridge: Harvard University Press.

Dunbar, *R.* (1998). The Social Brain Hypothesis. *Evolutionary Anthropology 6, no. 5*, pp. 178–190.

Elias, N. (2000). *The Civilizing Process. Sociogenetic and Psychogenetic Investigations*. Revised edition of 1994. Oxford: Basil Blackwell.

Freeman, W. (1995). *Societies of Brains. A Study in the Neuroscience of Love and Hate*. New Jersey: Laurence Erlbaum Associates, Hillsdale.

Freeman, W. (2001). *How Brains make up their Minds*. New York: Columbia University Press.

Gallese, V. (2001). The 'shared manifold' hypothesis: from mirror neurons to empathy. *Journal of Consciousness Studies. 8.5-7*, pp. 22-50.

Hobson, R. P. (1993). *Autism and the development of mind*. Hove, Sussex: Erlbaum.

Meares, R. (2000). *Intimacy and Alienation: Memory, Trauma and Personal Being*. London: Routledge.

Merleau-Ponty, M. (1945/1962). *Phenomenology of Perception*. Smith, C. (trans.). London: Routledge.

Pines, M. (1998). Reflections on Mirroring. In *Circular Reflections*. London: Jessica Kingsley.

Rizzolatti, G., & Arbib, M. (1998). Language within our grasp. *Trends in Neuroscience*. 21.5, pp. 188-194.

Rizzolatti, G., Fogassi, L., & Gallese, V. (2001). Neurophysiological mechanisms underlying the Understanding and Imitation of Action. *Nature Reviews Neuroscience* 2. (9), pp. 661-70.

Rothschild, E. (2001). *Economic Sentiments. Adam Smith, Condorcet and The Enlightenment.* Cambridge: Harvard University Press.

Smith, A. (1976) *The Wealth of Nations* . In R.H. Campbell & A.S. Skinner (Eds), *The Glasgow edition of the Works and Correspondence of Adam Smith, vol. 2.*

Wexler, B.E. (2006). *Brain and culture: neurobiology, ideology, and social change.* Cambridge: MIT Press.

Zinkin, L. (2000). *Exchange as a therapeutic factor in group analysis.* In D. Brown, & L. Zinkin (Eds) *The Psyche and the Social World Developments in Group Analytic Theory* London: Jessica Kingsley Publications.

In: The Other Side of the Coin
Editors: L. Brunori and M. Pines
ISBN: 978-1-62618-726-9

Chapter 4

MICROCREDIT AND POVERTY: A MULTI-DIMENSIONAL DEBATE

Alba Didem Özonaran*

Fundraising Department, UNHCR, Northern Italy

ABSTRACT

This chapter explores how is it possible to evaluate if Microcredit is an effective poverty reduction tool, defining poverty as a multi-dimensional concept.

The attempt is then to try to identify valuable criteria and questions to ask in order to evaluate Microcredit as poverty reduction tool, and then to 'test' those questions, using secondary information, in order to understand if they are valuable and appropriate for Microcredit, and which are the problems and issues related to their application.

The first part is about the definition of poverty. Poverty is going to be considered as a multi-dimensional phenomena (a condition of ill-being), in contraposition with the absence of poverty, the condition of well-being, with well-being characterized by different criteria regarding different aspect of the people's lives.

In order to avoid a strong top-down approach, the definition of poverty takes inspiration from two different sources. One is Chambers, who in 2006 proposed a model of development as movement from ill-being to well-being, with the dimension of well-being characterized by material well-being, reduction of vulnerability, empowerment and social

* Correspondence regarding this chapter may be addressed to *didem.ozonaran@gmail.com.*

inclusion. The other source is the work of Narayan (2000), which in his work reports the definition of the poor themselves about the condition of being poor. Moreover a fifth criteria is going to be considered, which is the sustainability of Microcredit in its form of group lending (in the Grameen way), fundamental condition for the life of any institution, and then for their capacity to deliver services.

After the identification of the criteria some questions to ask in order to evaluate the effectiveness of Microcredit for each criteria are going to be identified and tested, to see if they are effective to evaluate if Microcredit can reduce poverty. The case study analyzed is Bangladesh, as the focus of this book is the group, and group lending' Microcredit widely diffused in this country.

At the end of the analysis of the criteria almost all the question asked seems to be relevant if we are willing to measure the impact of Microcredit, but what emerges is that in the criteria characterized by subjectivity what is needed is a more participatory approach, with question to be asked directly to the beneficiaries of Microcredit, to better understand their experiences and their feelings regarding the changes that this tool has made in their life.

INTRODUCTION

This chapter is based on my final dissertation made at the end of the MSc: 'Development and Planning: Social Development Practice', University College of London.

The concept of poverty has developed in the last decades, especially since it has become the principal focus of development interventions. From a starting uni-dimensional definition of poverty, nowadays poverty is generally agreed to be multi-dimensional, touching different aspects of people's lives.

This development underlines the importance of the identification and evaluation of poverty reduction tools, as Microcredit was often considered to be.

Microcredit is claimed to be a panacea for the reduction of poverty. Several authors have focused their researches on demonstrating how Microcredit is effective, or how it is not, on reducing poverty. These surveys and papers are approaching their research from different perspectives and points of view, achieving often completely different results.

The understanding of the efficacy of Microcredit in the fight against poverty is fundamental, as this should be the basis over which promote the expansion of its use.

The aim of this chapter is then to explore how is it possible to evaluate if Microcredit is an effective poverty reduction tool, defining poverty as a multi-dimensional concept.

MICROCREDIT AND POVERTY

Key Debates on Microcredit

The development of Microfinance and its diffusion around the world however created different models and different approaches, considering it from different perspectives. Mayoux (2000) for example underlines three different paradigms.

The first is the Poverty Alleviation paradigm, which rationale is that Microfinance is an effective tool for the "alleviation of poverty and vulnerability and increasing well-being for the poorest households." (Mayoux, 2000, p. 6). This paradigm is often criticized as the small amount of the loan is considered not enough in order to alleviate poverty, and the repayment of the loan is considered a new stress increasing the vulnerability of the poor.

The second is the Empowerment paradigm, which rationale considers Microfinance as an entry point for economic, social and political empowerment, especially for women. The criticism of this model is generally focused on the fact that Microcredit is not producing real effects on empowerment. We are going to discuss deeply this later.

The third is the Financial Sustainability paradigm, which rationale is that financial sustainable programs "increase access to micro-finance services for large numbers of poor people" (Ibid.).

This paradigm seems to be one of the most criticized, as following the sustainability approach several different institutions provide loan with high interest rates, making worse the situation of those accessing to credit and losing the social issue of this tool.

Another criticism often made and relevant to this paper is the one about the methodology of group lending. In fact the methodology of group lending is often criticized as "attending group meetings and monitoring group members can be too costly, especially where houses are not close together." (Aghion & Morduch, 2000, p. 4).

What is Poverty? Conceptual Framework

After this introduction on what Microcredit is and how it works, it is fundamental to understand what poverty is and what it means, and how is going to be approached in this paper.

The poverty debate has characterized the past few decades of development discussion. From a generally agreed definition of poverty based on income, the analysis and understanding of poverty has been enriched over the years. The debate is really important, as poverty has become the primary focus of development interventions.

The definition of poverty is fundamental for several reasons. Defining poverty is in fact the basis over which every organization, government and institution focused on development, base its policy and its intervention, and decides the tools to use for poverty reduction. As mentioned by Ruggeri & co. definitions "have different implications for policy, and also for targeting since they identify different people as being poor" (Ruggeri, 2006, p.10).

Historically speaking the definition of poverty has changed over time. As mentioned above "historically speaking poverty has been related to income, which remains at the core of the concept today" (Townsend, 2006, p. 5). In fact in the 60's the analysis of poverty was focused on income, particularly looking at indicators as the GNP (Gross National Product). The emphasis was then given to growth and "poverty alleviation was rather a side effect of growth and assumed to trickle down of its benefit" (Gerster, 1999, p.3).

In the past few decades the analysis of poverty was enriched in particular by several innovations. In the 70's Townsend in his work with Runciman introduced the concept of relative deprivation. Townsend in particular redefined poverty as something related to the context, so "not just as a failure to meet minimum nutrition or subsistence levels, but rather as a failure to keep up with the standards prevalent in a given society."(Maxwell, 1999, p. 3).

So poverty was defined as inadequate resources to allow people to participate in activities which are customary in the societies in which they live, so in this view poverty is related to the social context. This was in contrast with what mentioned in the beginning of the 19th century by Rowentree and Booth, who talked about absolute poverty as the failure to satisfy subsistence needs, being then not a relative concept, but a more concrete one.

The second important innovation came by the ILO's definition of poverty as lack of basic needs. The concept of basic needs is a broad view of poverty, including not just income as measurement, but also other aspect, as those provided within society. Poverty then was defined as "lack of access to health, education and other services" (Maxwell, 1999, p.4).

Finally the debate on social exclusion. The concept of social exclusion evolved, arriving to a definition of it as "on multiple deprivation (low income, poor housing, poor access to education and health), but also on the process by which multiple deprivation occurs. The key arenas for exclusion include democratic and legal systems, markets, welfare state provisions, and family and community: rights, resources and relationships are all important." (Maxwell, 1999, p. 4).

The 80's are characterized by several studies that deepened the understanding of poverty. First of all, the work of Chambers and his focus on participation added complexity on the analysis and understanding of poverty. Chambers underlined the importance of participation of the poor in the definition of poverty itself, introducing the idea of poverty as a subjective experience. Indeed in his work he underlined the participation of people itself in development as fundamental. Following the work of Chambers, participatory researches lead "to a new interest in vulnerability, and its counterpart, security, associated with better understanding of seasonality and of the impact of shocks, notably drought. This pointed to the importance of assets as buffers, and also to social relations (the moral economy, social capital)." (Maxwell, 1999, p. 3). The concept of vulnerability went further in the work of the UNDP and DFID, to the broad concept of livelihood and the creation of the sustainable livelihood framework.

In the 80's Sen defined poverty as capability deprivation, being capabilities what a person can do or be. So here poverty is intended as capability deprivation meaning the lack of "the substantive freedoms he or she enjoys to lead the kind of life he or she has reason to value."(Alkire, 2005, p. 2). In this view the poor are then those without the possibility to achieve something, with lack of opportunities. "Development can be seen, it is argued here, as a process of expanding the real freedoms that people enjoy." (Alkire, 2005, p. 2).

The 80's were then characterized by several studies of gender, especially looking at gender relations. The gender analysis helped on the development of the concept of poverty as powerlessness, meaning a lack of power in several different aspects of life, and the related focus on empowerment as way of getting out of poverty, also following the pioneeristic work of Freire in the 70's.

The 90's added new ideas in developing the notion of poverty. "The idea of well-being came to act as a metaphor for absence of poverty, with concomitant emphasis on how poor people themselves view their situation." (Maxwell, 1999, p. 3). At the same time, inspired by Sen, UNDP developed the idea of human development: "the denial of opportunities and choices… to lead a long, healthy, creative life and to enjoy a decent standard of living, freedom, dignity, self-esteem and the respect of others." (UNDP, 1997, in Maxwell, 1999, p. 4).

As mentioned by Vandemoortele: "The poverty debate has not been settled" (Vandemoortele, 2006). In fact from a money metric uni-dimensional view as the one of income, the poverty debate has enriched the understanding of poverty during the past 30 years with several different definitions and approaches. But the debate is still open, and despite the rich discussion, income is still the main criteria used for measuring poverty.

The World Bank for example defines poverty as lack of income and uses reference lines set at $1 and $2 per day. This definition is still commonly accepted, with poverty view as economic deprivation. The World Bank is then focused on income as measurement of poverty, and on increasing income as way of reducing poverty. But as mentioned by Edward "The basis for the $1 a day poverty line […] is not derived from any consideration of well-being or basic needs" (Edward, 2006, p.14), and in general the major criticism of this definition of poverty is that it is reductive and not adapt to capture the complexity of this phenomena.

Other institutions instead define poverty in a more complex way. Oxfam for example states in its website: "Oxfam's definition of poverty goes beyond the purely economic to encompass capabilities, powerlessness and inequality". The focus of Oxfam is then not just on increasing income, but especially promoting human rights and empowering people.

The Grameen Bank, one of the major Microfinance institution, evaluate poverty through 10 different indicators, including income and money related indicators but also access to water, access to primary education, adequate clothing, use of sanitary latrine, 3 meals a day and adequate healthcare. (Yunus, 2006). The focus of this institution is then on increasing income but also on the basic needs of its beneficiaries.

The definition of an organization is fundamental because, as mentioned before "they do have different implications for policy and also for targeting since they identify different people as being poor" (Ruggeri, 2006, p.10). For example BRAC, the second biggest provider of Microcredit in Bangladesh, in its website states: "BRAC approaches poverty alleviation with a holistic approach". This is reflected on their operational approach to poverty reduction, as we can see in their annual report, where they look at health and nutrition, education, environment, governance and social development (see report 2004 and 2007) in order to evaluate their achievements. The debate on poverty has underlined the complexity of this phenomenon that makes it difficult nowadays to approach it in a uni-dimensional way. This would reduce its complexity and the effectiveness of every intervention aspiring to reduce poverty, and that is why a multi-dimensional approach is needed. The World Bank states: "poverty is a lack of opportunities, powerlessness, and vulnerability. Poverty is truly a multidimensional phenomenon in such a setting and requires multi-dimensional policy and program interventions in order to improve the well-being of individuals and, hence, make them free from poverty."

Development as good change - from ill-being to well-being

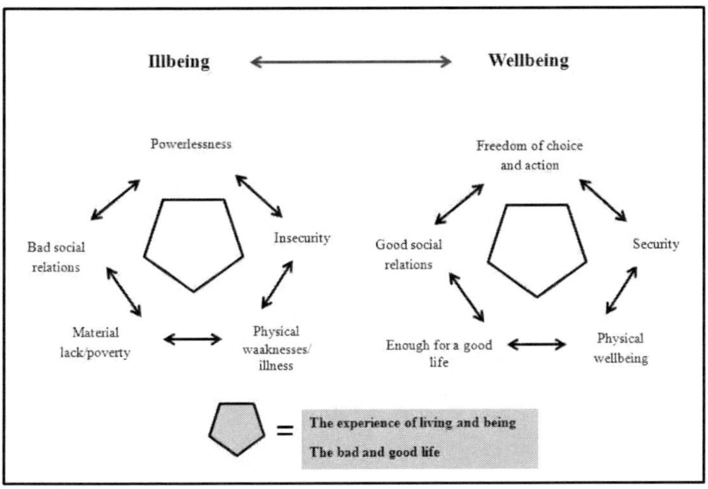

Chambers, 2006.

Figure 1. Development as good change.

Again according to the World Bank (World Bank 2000), "poverty is pronounced deprivation in well-being". Also Gerster states "poverty is the opposite of well-being" (Gerster, 1999, p.4). Following the literature we decided to use an approach to poverty as lack of well-being, considering well-being as multidimensional as: "Poverty defined as a lack of well-being is clearly multidimensional" (Edward, 2006, p. 14). Well-being itself is a very difficult concept to define. Narayan, in its participatory analysis of the meaning of poverty states "When poor people speak about well-being, they speak about the material, social, physical, psychological, and spiritual dimensions, in addition to security and the freedom of choice and action. Conversely, poverty and ill-being are the lack of material well-being, insecurity, social isolation, psychological distress, and lack of freedom of choice and action." (Narayan, 2000). The change from ill-being to well-being is in this analysis conceived as development, inspired by Chambers. Looking at the table aside the author shows: "five dimensions to illustrate development as good change. Development thus can be seen as shifting from ill-being to well-being, with interventions to enhance well-being possible at any of the five points" (Chambers, 2006, p.3). As is possible to see from the definitions of Narayan and Chambers above, the criteria of material lack, insecurity, social isolation and lack of freedom of choice and action are repeated by both authors as fundamental areas of concern, that are key factors from the ill-being to the well-being of a person. Chambers in his analysis underlines the limitation of every kind of definition and analysis coming from "our analysis and views". (Chambers, 2006, p. 3). He underlines the necessity to approach poverty form a perspective of subjectivity, hearing the voice of the people, and indicates in the work of Narayan a way to integrate 'our' understanding and analysis with the one of the poor.

This double repetition, from the top to the bottom and back, gives the strength to 4 of the criteria we are going to use in order to analyze the effectiveness of Microcredit on poverty reduction: material lack, powerlessness, vulnerability and social exclusion. The fifth criteria chosen is sustainability, which is not directly related to reduction of poverty itself, but is a fundamental basement for the life of Microcredit institution, and thus for its possibility to deliver its services.

The Criteria

Material Well-Being

Material well-being is defined by Chambers in its table as "having enough for a good life", in contrast with material lack/poverty. Narayan mentions that people talk about the material dimension of poverty, looking at poverty again as lack of material well-being. Generally speaking a useful mean to have enough for a good life is money, and there are two common ways of measuring how much money people do have. The first is measuring their income, that is for example the way adopted by the World Bank, which defines its poverty lines based on income, of 1 $ a day or 2 $ a day, and this is going to be the first tool to use to measure if Microcredit is helping people on having enough for a good life.

Despite the easiness of measuring income, this criteria is often criticized as inconsistent, as it does not consider other 'money-related' aspects as debts or savings. Indeed income is important but still not enough in order to measure poverty, while household consumption seems more appropriate to evaluate a poverty reduction tool. Income seems "a mean to an end" (Kakwani, 2006, p.20), more than an end itself. Household consumption is the amount of money spent on food and other goods and services, and in this case it is a useful tool as it can help us on understanding if a household has enough liquidity to spend on what is necessary for a good life. In this sense household consumption seems to be a more sensible tool than income. To achieve a more complete overview of how Microcredit improves the material well-being of its beneficiaries we are going to look at both the measurement. The first measurement is income, to understand if microcredit has a positive impact on the income of its beneficiaries, and the second criteria is household consumption, as it seems that those indicators together can help to understand if participation to Microcredit programs leads to more available resources to spend in order to achieve a better life. The questions that have to be asked in order to evaluate the effectiveness of Microcredit in this aspect of poverty reduction are then:

- Has the income of the beneficiaries increased after accessing to Microcredit?
- Is the household consumption of the beneficiaries increased after accessing to Microcredit?

Vulnerability

"Vulnerability [...] means defenselessness, insecurity, exposure to risk, shocks, stress." (Warren, 1995, p. 17). The dimension of Vulnerability has now a central role in development, as it is understood that is a key aspect of poverty. The DFID for example states "Vulnerability is a key dimension of poverty" (DFID, 2001, p.24); and Gerster "Reducing vulnerability is a priority" (Gerster, 1999, p.12). The definition of vulnerability is generally agreed in the literature "as the capacity to be wounded by a perturbation or stress in the natural or social environment. Put another way, vulnerability can be described as a lack of security from environmental threats. It results from a combination of processes that shape the degrees of exposure to an hazard, sensitivity to its stress and impacts, and resilience in the face of those effects." (SEI website). Vulnerability then is strictly related to insecurity, and "Insecurity is an important component of welfare and can be understood as vulnerability to a decline in well-being." (World Bank, *Measuring Poverty*). This is especially true for the poorest, that lacking of entitlements are morc sensible to risks and shocks. Looking at the sentence of Narayan and the table of Chambers in both the authors underline the dimension of insecurity, which seems to be a fundamental mean for evaluating the vulnerability of people. Indeed the literature underlines vulnerability as "exposure to risk, shocks and stresses" (Warren, 1995, p. 17). So the capacity of the beneficiaries to face those stresses and shocks should be another important dimension for evaluating the reduction of vulnerability. The questions that are important to do are then:

- Does Microcredit help on reducing the vulnerability (insecurity) of its beneficiaries?
- Does Microcredit help its beneficiaries on facing the stresses and shocks affecting their lives?

Dimensions of powerlessness and ill-being

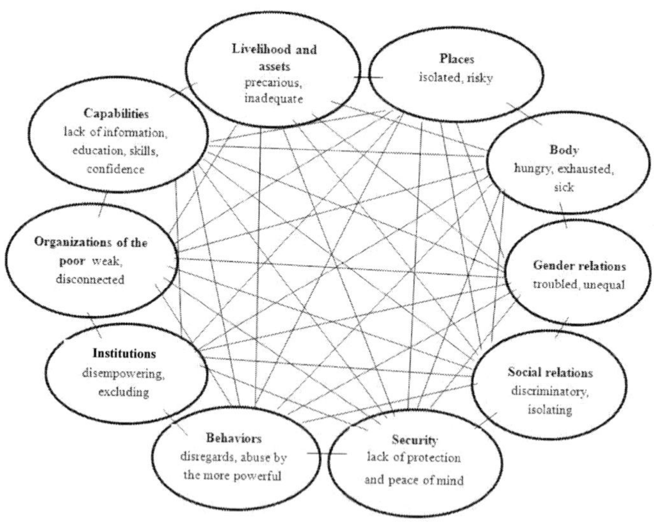

Narayan, 2000.

Figure 2. Dimensions of powerlessness and ill-being.

Empowerment

Powerlessness is recognized as a fundamental aspect of poverty. Narayan, for example, states in his work "Poor people's lives are characterized by powerlessness and voicelessness." (Narayan, 2000).

Powerlessness is characterized by several different aspects, which interrelate with each-others, as very well represented in the table next page.

As we can see "Powerlessness results from multiple, interlocking disadvantages, which, in combination, make it extremely difficult for poor people to escape poverty" (Narayan, 2000).

In fact the importance of reducing powerlessness is fundamental to fight poverty, and its relation with ill-being is underlined by the graph and also by Mayoux, that talks about empowerment as increased well-being (Mayoux, 2000, p. 5).

In order to help people escape from the circle of ill-being, empowerment is then fundamental.

Sen states that "Empowering the poor must be the starting point. Without empowerment poverty eradication is not possible and even efforts on poverty alleviation may not be sustainable" (Sen, 1997, p.180), underlining also the important aspect of sustainability, as empowering people is a long term investment in the sense of development, durable.

Being powerlessness a broad concept including several different aspects, the definition of empowerment may vary, but we will try to use broad definition that could include different aspects. Chambers talks about empowerment as "having freedom of choice and action" (Chambers 2006). The World Bank states "Empowerment means increasing the capacity of poor people to affect the decisions that have a bearing on their lives, by investing in them and by removing barriers that they face to engage in political, social and economic activities". (World Bank, Chapter 1). We can mix all the definitions above stating that empowerment means increasing the freedom of choice and actions that allow people to have control over the decisions that affect their lives.

Indeed the World Bank points out the barriers people face, that decrease their freedom. Those barriers are considered to be on political, social and economical activities. The questions to be asked to the beneficiaries should then be focused on understanding if Microcredit helps in removing some of those barriers that impede their freedom of choice and action.

The questions to ask are then:

- Are the participants feeling having more power in their lives?
- Are the beneficiaries having more freedom of choice and action in their lives?

Social Inclusion

Social exclusion is a very broad concept, including different aspects of people's lives. De Haan states that "it refers to exclusion (deprivation) in the economic, social and political sphere" (De Haan, 1999, p. 6). Silver in her article goes further, defining the process causing social exclusion. "Social exclusion is usually defined as a dynamic process of progressive multidimensional rupturing of 'social bound' at the individual and collective levels. By social bound I mean the social relations, institutions, and imagined identities of belonging constituting social cohesion, integration, or solidarity" (Silver, 2007, p.1).

Silver underlines the rupture of social bounds that creates social exclusion, mentioning social relation and institutions as social bounds. As already mentioned, Microcredit has been created in order to give the possibility of an inclusion in institutions for the poor normally excluded by them.

But another issue that should be considered is if it helps on reducing social exclusion by the creation of new and better relationships. In fact being part of institution like BRAC or the Grameen bank can lead to have access to a broader kind of relation, more intended in the social way. In fact "poverty and ill-being are the lack of material well-being, insecurity, social isolation" (Narayan, 2000), being social isolation an aspect of social exclusion.

So an important thing to look at is that if being part of those Microfinance institutions can help people from getting out of isolation, through creating new social channels and networks, fundamental aspect of the reduction of poverty in their lives. This is why to evaluate if Microcredit is helping people getting out of the poorness of isolation it is important to understand if it helps on creating new and better social relation.

The question to ask is then:

- Does Microcredit help people on having better relation and more social network?

Sustainability

Talking about sustainability in this paper, we refer to the financial sustainability, meaning the capacity of an institution to "avoid bankruptcy" (Ferro & Weber, 2006, p.4); meaning to avoid collapsing because of economic failure. This criteria is different from the others chosen, as it is not directly related to reduction of poverty, but it is fundamental for the life of Microcredit institutions, and then for their capacity to deliver services. As mentioned by Ferro and Weber, MFIs (Microfinance Institutions) "face a double challenge: not only they have to provide financial services for the poor *(outreach)*, but they also have to consider their cost to avoid bankruptcy *(sustainability)*" (Ferro & Weber, 2006, p. 4). So the sustainability of Microfinance institution is important for the *outreach* mentioned by Ferro and Weber, and in this sense is related to poverty, as it increases the chances of credit access for the poor. "The main argument to support this view is that large scale outreach to the poor on a long-term basis cannot be guaranteed if microfinance institutions are incapable of standing on their own feet" (Hermes and Lensink, 2007, p. 7). The importance of the financial sustainability of a Microcredit institution is recognized by several institutions focusing on "setting up self-sustainable micro-finance programmes which increase access to micro-finance services for a large number of poor people" (Mayoux, 2000, p. 6).

As mentioned by Khandker "A program's sustainability depends on the resources that microcredit program raise and control, on the repayment rate of the loans, and on the programs' institutional development" (Khandker, 1998, p. 84). As we can see repayment is part of this definition, and is one of the variables helping an institution being sustainable. "Improving the repayment rate could also help reduce the dependence on subsidies leading to a better sustainability level" (Godquin, 2002, p. 2).

Having high repayment rate is in the literature underlined as being important also for other factors. "High repayment rates may allow the MFI to lower the interest rate it charges to the borrower […] enabling more borrower to have access to credit", and "Repayment performance also acts as an important positive signal when the MFI has to rise new founds. […] For all these reasons, higher repayment rates are largely associated with benefit both for the MFI and the borrower". (Godquin, 2002, p. 2).

Following the discussion above, to analyze the repayment rate of Microcredit institution is important in order to allow this tool to deliver its services, as without good repayment rates the institution can risk bankruptcy (consequently the reduction of provision of the service), and higher interest rate for its beneficiaries, making their situation more difficult. So the guideline here is that if we want to measure if Microcredit can reduce poverty we need to look at its sustainable capacity to deliver services. This sustainable capacity is determined by several factors, being one of the most important the repayment rate, fundamental then to evaluate if Microcredit can reduce poverty. What seems to be important to see in this case, assumed that credit is a tool for poverty reduction, is that the particular form of group-lending provided by Microcredit institutions in Bangladesh is actually having good repayment rate, better than other kind of credit; if it is then better in the capacity to provide sustainable services thanks to higher repayment rates.

The question to ask is then:

- Is group lending having better repayment rates compared with other kind of lending?

Analysis of the Case Study

Poverty

Bangladesh is a poor country. Looking at the HDI for example, its position is the 140th (UNDP website), on the lowest side of the 'medium development' countries, and its 2007 per-capita GDP is $ 1,300 (CIA website).The economy of Bangladesh is heavily dependent on rural activities, and there is a high incidence of poverty, higher in rural areas than urban. As mentioned by Khandker "50% of the rural population still lives below the poverty line" (Khandker, 1998, p.18). However the situation in the last few decades seems to have improved slowly and someone claims the success of Microcredit to explain this trend.

The Women's Situation

Among the poor in rural Bangladesh, women are heavily dependent on men. In fact the systems of *purdah*, "the practice of secluding and protecting women to uphold social standards of modesty and morality" (Hashemi et al, 1996, p.1730) leads to the isolation and subordination of women. Because of the norm of *purdah* women are usually interacting within the household, and their social relations outside the family are very limited and often forbidden. "These social norms curtail women's involvement in market transactions and constrain their potential to generate incomes, reinforcing their economic dependence." (Ibid.). In Bangladesh men control the resources and how those are to be spent, with a strong preference on boy's education and care. The education of girls is considered not necessary, and they are the ones denied of food for first in case of famine, and of health care in case of illness. The gravity of this situation is demonstrated by the mortality rate of men and women in Bangladesh, where the trend is the opposite respect the majority of the countries of the world, with the life expectancy being lower for women than men.

Seasonality

Being Bangladesh principally a rural country, with the majority of the poor living in those areas, the condition of the poorest is heavily dependent on agricultural labor. "The weather-induced seasonality of the crop cycle is the major source of seasonality of labor use and income flows in Bangladesh" (Khandker, 1998, p. 50).

The Bangladeshi agricultural labor demand is dropping dramatically in the low season, creating a difficult situation, with a high degree of unemployment and the related dropping of income of the poorest, that in this season are struggling for survival.

INSTITUTIONS IN BANGLADESH

The specific focus in this book is Microcredit in the Grameen way, meaning in its form of a group loan. In Bangladesh after the Grameen Bank, with more than 1 million members, BRAC is the second biggest provider of Microcredit. Another important provider is "the Rural Development Project-12 (RD-12) of the Bangladesh Rural Development Board (BRDB), with about 0.5 million members." (Khandker, 1998, p. 4). Both programs use group-based credit schemes to target women and the poor, that are defined in all the programs (Grameen as well) as those who own less than half acre of land.

Despite some differences, the common issue among those Microcredit institutions is that they are providing credit through collateral free group loan, and that they are following the ideas that in order to reduce poverty credit is essential. "In Bangladesh, the poor have traditionally been denied access to the formal banking system, as they are unable to provide collateral for loans and typically deal in small amounts of money. This means that they have few opportunities to save, borrow and invest. Moneylenders in the informal credit markets charge very high interest rates which also restricts people's access to credit. We believe that making credit, which can be invested in productive activity, universally available is essential in reducing poverty." (BRAC's Annual Report 2007, p. 17).

ANALYSIS OF THE CRITERIA

The majority of the surveys analyzed for this paper are from electronic journals. Unfortunately this research has been limited by the difficulty to find some survey made by Bangladeshi institutions or researchers, not always available. Indeed several surveys used are a bit out of date, being from the end of the 90's. This seems to reflect the fact that, after its creation in the 70's, the 80's were characterized by the 'discovering' of Microcredit, and particularly the 90's by the worldwide interest in this tool, with a consequent huge amount of survey made in order to evaluate its effectiveness.

However we tried to diversify this research and to use pertinent material from relevant sources.

Material Well-Being

The relevance of income as way of measurement of the effectiveness of Microcredit seems to be not confirmed by the literature. In fact the scarcity of data about this criteria seems to underline the structural problems of the criteria itself. As already mentioned, income is difficult to measure, as there are several different factors that might disturb its measurement, as savings, debts and so on. This is especially true when it comes to measure an increase on income of participants of Microcredit, where the credit is given in order to generate and improve a business, where the income might be invested, as generally strongly suggested by Microcredit operators. Despite the importance of income as way of measurement of poverty, this criteria seems to not fit with Microcredit and our analysis for the reasons above.

About Household consumption the conclusion seems to be different. Despite some criticism, the majority of the survey analyzed use household consumption as a way of measurement of the material well-being of the beneficiaries of Microcredit, showing a positive impact of it. The question chosen seems then sensible and effective, better than the one on income. This is probably due to the fact that consumption needs are primary needs, needs not always satisfied in poor households. Probably when there is an increase of resources in the household, those resources are directed for first to those primary needs, important for the well-being of a household. Household consumption seems then a sensible criteria in order to evaluate the material well-being of the beneficiaries.

Reduction of Vulnerability

As mentioned in the introduction to Bangladesh, seasonality seems to be the most important factor affecting the lives of Bangladeshi population. In fact "strong seasonality of crop production is well known to affect the timing of income flows […] Agricultural employment also responds to seasonal variation in the demand for labor in various crop-related activities" (Pitt and Khandker, 1998, pp. 13-14). The problem related to different seasons seems then probably one of the biggest risk and shocks for Bangladeshi people. The low season is characterized as the period of major stress for them, when they're more vulnerable, as this period means less employment, then less income, less food, less consumption. So, in order to understand if Microcredit decreases the level of insecurity of its participant in the particular case of Bangladesh, it is relevant to see if it helps people on facing the problem of seasonality.

More specifically, what emerges from the statements above is that the two major problems in this period are labor variability and income flows due to labor flow. Looking at the literature about this matter the majority of the surveys based on Bangladesh try to understand if Microcredit has an effect on the reduction of vulnerability through evaluating if it helps on smoothing consumption and labor. I will embrace those two specific problems, as are related to my general questions on vulnerability.

The questions important to be asked are then:

- Does microcredit help beneficiaries on smoothing consumption?
- Does microcredit help on differentiate labor supply of its beneficiaries?

The question if Microcredit helps on reducing the vulnerability of its beneficiaries seems to be relevant in order to evaluate Microcredit as a poverty reduction tool, but if we look specifically at the two different questions made in order to evaluate if Microcredit can help to reduce poverty in the specific case of Bangladesh, some problems seem to emerge.

The question about the smoothened consumption through the year seems to be a good question, especially if we assume that consumption is one of the primary needs of a household. Khandker for example seems to show that frequently poor people decide to access to Microcredit in order to reduce their vulnerability, with a higher credit demand in low season.

However a frequent criticism made about Microcredit is that it can lead to an increased vulnerability due to the stress of the repayment of the loan, and none of the surveys founded seem to discuss this subject. In fact all the survey analyzed have a strong top-down approach, with the conclusions made on the basis of the ideas of the authors. What emerges for example is that the diversification of labor is assumed to be helpful on the reduction of vulnerability, but this is not controlled. Different assets and different labors can lead to decreased vulnerability, but also to an increased amount of it. Having different labors in fact can be cause of an increased stress, as for example there can be the fear of failure of a business where some money have been invested, or because of the increase amount of working hours. What should be done in order to better evaluate the vulnerability of people is a more subjective approach of it. After having accessed Microcredit do they feel less vulnerable? Do they feel more able to face shocks and stresses? Vulnerability is a subjective experience, depending on different things, what is needed is then a more participative approach, with deeper interviews with the beneficiaries, asking them if they feel more able to face problems and shocks, and if they feel that the insecurity of their lives has decreased after accessing Microcredit. This could give a more complete understanding of the impact of Microcredit in the lives of its beneficiaries. The questions about vulnerability are then relevant, and even the top-down approach of the survey analyzed can give us important information, but those questions should be completed with questions to be asked directly to the beneficiaries.

Empowerment

About empowerment almost all the surveys based on Bangladesh analyze empowerment form a gender perspective. Mahmud states that "The condition of empowerment is defined as set of choices and options initially available to women for increasing welfare and reducing subordination to men" (Mahmud, 2003, p. 586), and this is particularly true in Bangladesh where, because of the norm of *purdah,* women are affected by discriminatory gender relations; they have some social barriers that makes them powerlessness, in society as well as in the household.

Indeed the majority of the beneficiaries of Microcredit in Bangladesh are women, with some institutions working exclusively with them. This is why I am going to adapt my question about empowerment to a gender perspective, using women as example to see if Microcredit is empowering its beneficiaries. My first question is:

- Are the participants feeling having more power in their lives?

Being the lives of women often confined in the household, where the household power relationship is one of the biggest problems, an important question to ask is if having access to Microcredit increased their power in the household; the question will be then:

- Are the women participant having more power in the household?

Indeed about the second question, instead of asking about the freedom of choice and action of the beneficiaries in general, I will look at the freedom of choice and action of women beneficiaries, to see if this question is relevant in order to understand if Microcredit has an impact on it.

The use of the question about control over loan in order to understand the effectiveness of Microcredit on empowerment of women, particularly in the intra-household relationship is not relevant until we do not use a comparison group of not participants, trying to understand the different control over resources in general of women participant and non-participant.

Indeed the fact that the control over loan is an index of empowerment seems to be again a top-down assumption, as represented by the fact that several authors underline that having access to credit itself, even without control over loan, improves the condition of women, as they are seen as income generator. The surveys reporting those results are based on the statement of women participant, reporting about their condition before and after loan. This kind of investigation, with the perspective of the women themselves, results then to be the more sensible and valuable in order to understand the change in the intra-household relationship, a variable that is difficult to analyze otherwise.

The question about the empowering effect of Microcredit is relevant, but being the change in the intra-household relationship something really difficult to measure from objective criteria, what should be done is to ask women beneficiaries if they feel empowered in their intra-household relationship after accessing to Microcredit.

About the second question, all the surveys examined looked at several different aspects of the lives of women in Bangladesh, showing that women participating in Microcredit programs are better performing than non-participant groups. The approach to this question is easier than the previous one, as the freedom of a woman can be more easily compared with the one of other woman, and evaluated using objective criteria.

The question about the freedom of choice and action of women beneficiaries as indicator of the empowerment of women seems to be largely agreed as being important in order to understand the effectiveness of Microcredit on the empowerment of women, indeed the results of all the survey analyzed seems to agree affirmatively, showing better results for women participating on Microcredit programs in comparison with not participants, thing that seems to underline that this question is valuable and sensible in order to evaluate the effectiveness of Microcredit.

Social Inclusion

The question about social inclusion of the beneficiaries of Microcredit has been adopted by different authors, all of them reporting positive answers. Here again the focus is on women and on their relationships before and after accessing Microcredit. The results seems to show that the question postulate is effective, particularly in Bangladesh, where the relationships of women are often confined on their husband's kinship because of the norm of *purdah*, in a context then where the isolation seems to be a characteristic of the life of the majority of poor women. In this context the fact that Microcredit can help on creating social network is really important, as it breaks some of the cultural barriers due to the norm of *purdah*, giving women a chance to increase their network outside the family, with more social relation, and increasing their social support, with better social relation.

The question seems then valuable and sensible in order to understand if Microcredit can reduce poverty, on the particular aspect of the social exclusion, and in order to understand if it can produce good social relations.

Sustainability

Despite the claim about the impressive high repayment rates of the group lending approach, it has been difficult to find surveys comparing this approach with other ways of lending. The comparison between individual and group lending seems to have different results in the words of Khandker that however does not report any data, and in the findings of Britton, that unfortunately are made considering a different case study, Zimbabwe, making it difficult to compare and discuss the results.

However, in the survey of Sharma and Zeller the answer to our question is affirmative, showing a huge difference between the high repayment performance of Microcredit institutions and the lowest performance of commercial banks in Bangladesh. From their survey it seems then that Microcredit is having better repayment rates than commercial Banks in Bangladesh, with a bigger chance of it to achieve sustainability and then a durable provision of service for its participants.

The high repayment rate of the group lending reported in the literature and the better performance of it compared to the formal commercial banks seems to confirm that this tool is characterized by the fact that having good repayment rate might achieve a long term sustainability and then a durable provision of its services, with less risk of having bankruptcy. This aspect is really important if we assume that Microcredit is a poverty reduction tool, and that its collapse can deprive its beneficiaries from an important source of well-being.

CONCLUSION

After testing the questions created in order to measure if Microcredit can reduce poverty the results are different.

Regarding the question about the impact on the material well-being of its beneficiaries what emerges is that income seems to not be an appropriate measurement in order to evaluate the effectiveness of Microcredit, probably due to the fact that it does not consider other money related aspects as saving and debts, and also because of the tool we were analyzing, Microcredit, as the participants of it are often suggested to invest their income to improve their business, thing that makes it difficult to measure the effective increase of income before and after accessing Microcredit.

The result is different for Household consumption, which seems to be more sensible and appropriate as it shows a real increase on the expenditures of the beneficiaries of Microcredit. This is probably due to the fact that the expenditure on consumption are the one where for first some money is invested when there is an increase in the resources of a household. Overall then, the question about household consumption seems appropriate in order to see if Microcredit has an impact on the material well-being of its beneficiaries.

About vulnerability, while the question asked seems to be important in order to evaluate the reduction of the vulnerability of its beneficiaries, what seems to be a strong pattern is a top down approach, with no interest in beneficiaries' perspective. What emerges from the analysis is then that direct questions to the beneficiaries should be added, asking them if Microcredit had an impact on their vulnerability.

About empowerment what emerges is, again, the need of a participatory approach to this kind of evaluation, especially when we look at subjective experience as the vulnerability mentioned above and the power in the intra-household relationship. The perspective of the women themselves results then fundamental, and the question to ask should be then if they feel empowered in their intra-household relationship after accessing to Microcredit.

The second question on the contrary seems valuable, as the freedom of choice and action can be more easily compared with the one of women non participant in Microcredit programs, using indicators adapted to the context of Bangladesh. The question seems then important and valuable in order to evaluate the effect of Microcredit.

The question about social inclusion seems important too. The fact that all the surveys analyzed report that the women themselves mention that they are having more and better relationships shows us an important contribute on the aspect of 'having good relations' mentioned by Chambers when talking about social exclusion. The question seems then valuable and sensible in order to understand if Microcredit can reduce poverty on this particular aspect.

About sustainability the literature claims high repayment rate of the group lending and there are data confirming its better performance if compared to the formal commercial banks. The question seems then relevant if we assume that Microcredit can reduce poverty, and that its collapse can deprive its beneficiaries from an important source of well-being.

As we can see almost all the question asked seems to be relevant if we are willing to measure the impact of Microcredit, but what emerges is that in criteria characterized by subjectivity as the one of vulnerability and of the intra-household relationship what is needed is a more participatory approach, with question to be asked directly to the beneficiaries of Microcredit, to better understand their experiences and their feelings regarding the changes that this tool has made in their life.

This could give us a more complete understanding of this tool and its effects, difficult to measure if we take into consideration only a perspective from the 'top'. This is one important thing emerging from this paper, and this is an important reflection that should be used in future when willing to evaluate Microcredit.

Indeed another problem emerges. If we assume that Microcredit is effective on reducing poverty, with the huge amount of people participating in Bangladesh in such kind of program, we should expect an overall reduction of poverty in this country, with evident achievement. Unfortunately Bangladesh is still a really poor country, and the impact of Microcredit in this sense seems to not be as big as we could expect.

This result seems to demonstrate that actually Microcredit cannot reduce poverty.

So how we can combine this result with the general affirmation of the surveys analyzed, which often demonstrate a positive effect on the lives of its beneficiaries? The answer seems to be hidden in our analysis, which decided to evaluate Microcredit as tool in the road from the ill-being to the well-being of its beneficiaries. In this road Microcredit can have an active role, helping people achieving better life condition, but its role is still marginal, effective on a small scale, meaning looking at the individual and household level; its role is confined at the Micro level, as its name seems to evoke.

At the Macro level other measures should be taken, in order to create better condition for a country as Bangladesh, which without some changes will always struggle in its road for development. What Microcredit can do in this situation is to help its population in their day by day life, waiting and hoping for a better future.

References

Aghion, B., & Morduch, J. (2000). Microfinance Beyond Group Lending. *Economics of Transition, Vol. 8, No. 2,* pp. 401-420

Alkire, S. (2005). *Briefing Note Capability and Functionings: Definition & Justification*, HDCA.

Amin, R., Hill, R., & Yiping, L.; (1995). Does microcredit reach the poor and vulnerable? Evidence form northern Bangladesh. *Journal of Development Economics, N.70*, p. 59-82.

BRAC Annual Report 2004. http://www.brac.net/downloads_files/BRAC_Report_2004.pdf

BRAC Annual Report 2007. http://www.brac.net/downloads_files/BRAC_Annual_Report_2007.pdf

Chambers, R. (2006). What is poverty? Who asks? Who answers? In *Poverty in Focus N.9*,International Poverty Centre, UNDP, pp. 3-4.

De Haan, A. (1999). *Social Exclusion: towards an holistic understanding of deprivation*. London: DFID

Dowla, A. (2006). In Credit We Trust: Building Social Capital by Grameen Bank in Bangladesh. *Journal of Socio-Economics, 35, no. 1*, pp.102-22.

Evans, T., Adams, A., & Mohammed, R. (1999). Demystifying Nonparticipation in Microcredit: A Population-Based Analysis. *World Development, Vol. 27, No.2*, pp. 419-430.

Ferro, G., & Weber, S. (2006). *Measuring performance of Microfinance Institutions*, Cahier de recherché, HEG (Haute ècole de Geneve), CRAG (Centre de Recherche Appliquée en Gestion), Genève.

Fukuda-Parr, S. (2006). *The Human Poverty Index: A multidimensional measure*, in Poverty. In *Focus N.9*, International Poverty Centre, UNDP, pp. 3-4.

Gerster, R. (1999). *Alternative Approaches to Poverty Reduction Strategies*, Commisioned by The World Bank and Operations Evaluation Department, Richterswil (Switzerland).

Godquin, M. (2002). Microfinance repayment performance in Bangladesh: How to improve the allocation of loans by MFIs? *World Development, Vol. 32, No.11*, pp.1909-1926.

Goetz, A. M., & Sen Gupta, R. (1996). Who Takes the Credit? Gender, Power and Control Over Loan Use in Rural Credit Programs in Bangladesh. *World Development, Vol.24, No.1,* pp. 45-64.

Goldberg, N. (2005). *Measuring the Impact of Microfinance: Taking Stock of What We Know*, Grameen Foundation USA Publication Series, Washington DC.

Grameen Bank, *"2005 Annual Report"*. Dhaka:Grameen Bank,.

Greeley, M. (2006). Microfinance Impact and the MDGs: The challenge of scaling up. *IDS Working paper 255*, Brighton, UK.

Grieco, M. (1998). *Meeting the moment: Microfinance and the social exclusion agenda*, The Change Page, Accounting SIG, Business School, University of North London.

Hashemi, S. M., Schuler, S. R., & Riley, A. P. (1996). Rural Credit Programs and Women's Empowerment in Bangladesh. *World Development, Vol. 24, No.4*, pp.635-654.

Hermes, N., & Lensink, R. (2007). The empirics of Microfinance: what do we know? *The Economic Journal, 117,* F1-F10.

Hulme, D., Moore, K., & Shepherd, A. (2001). *Chronic poverty: meanings and analytical framework*, IDPM, CPRC working Paper 2.

Kakawani, N., & Son, H. (2006). Women's earning power and well being. *One Pager N.19,* International Poverty Centre (IPC), Brazil.

Khandker, S.R. (1998) *Fighting poverty with Microcredit*. Oxford: Oxford University press.

Khandker, S.R. (2003). Micro-Finance and Poverty- Evidence Using Panel Data from Bangladesh. *Policy Research Working Paper 2945*, The World Bank Development Research Group.

Larance, L.Y. (1998). *Building Social Capital from the Center: A Village-Level Investigation of Bangladesh's Grameen Bank*, Grameen Trust working paper.

Magner, M. (2007). *Microfinance: A Platform for Social Change*, Grameen Foundation Publication Series.

Mahmud, S. (2003). Actually How Empowering is Microcredit? *Development and Change, Vol.34, No.4*, pp. 577-605.

Matin, I. (2004). *The very poor who participate on microfinance institution and those who never did: A Comparative Analysis*, Research and Evaluation Division, BRAC.

Mayoux, L. (2000). Micro-finance and empowerment of women- A review of key issues. *Working Paper No.23,* ILO, Geneva.

Maxwell, S. (1999). *The meaning and Measurement of poverty*. ODI Poverty Briefing.

Miller, S. (1996). *The great chain of poverty explanations.* In E. Oyen & S. Miller (Eds) *Poverty: A global review*. Scandinavian University Press, pp.569-586

Murdoch, J. (1998). *Does Microfinance Really Help the poor? New evidence from Flagship Programs in Bangladesh.* Manuscript, Princeton University.

Narayan, D. (2000). Poverty Is Powerlessness and Voicelessness. *Finance and Development, Volume 37*, N.4, IMF.

Oxfam website (Last Accessed the 2nd of August 2008). http://www.oxfam.org.uk/

Pitt, M., & Khandker, S. (1998). Credit Programs for the Poor and Seasonality in Rural Bangladesh. *Journal of Development Studies, Vol.39, No. 2*, pp.1-24.

Ruggeri Laderchi, C., Saith, R., & Steward, F. (2003). Does the Definition of Poverty Matters? Comparing four approaches. *In Poverty in Focus N.9*, International Poverty Centre, UNDP, pp. 3-4.

Satya, R. (2002). Multi-dimensional poverty orderings. *DELTA and The World Bank, Working Paper 2002-22*, Calcutta: Chakravarty Indian Statistical Institute.

SEI (Stockholm Environment Institute) website (Last Accessed the 2nd of August 2008). http://sei-international.org/

Sen, A. (1997). Empowerment as an Approach to Poverty. *Poverty and Human Development*, Human Development Papers, UNDP, New York, pp. 175-194.

Sharma, M., & Zeller, M. (1997). Repayment Performance in Group-Based Credit Programs in Bangladesh: An Empirical Analysis. *World Development, Vol.25, No.10*, pp. 1731-1742.

Silver, H. (2007). The process of social exclusion: the dynamics of an evolving concept. CPRC *Working Paper 95*, Rhode Island, USA: Department of Sociology, Brown University.

Townsend, P. (2006). What is Poverty? An Historical Perspective. In *Poverty in Focus N.9*,International Poverty Centre, UNDP, pp. 3-4.

UNDP, (1997). *Human Development Report.*

Vandemoortele, J. (2006). Ending world poverty: is the debate settled? *One Pager N.12,* Brazil: International Poverty Centre.

Wratten, E. (1995). *Conceptualizing urban poverty. Environment and Urbanization, Vol. 7, No.1*, pp 12-18.

World Bank (2008). *Chapter 1. The Concept of Poverty and Well-being* (Last accessed the 2nd of August 2008). http://info.worldbank.org/etools/docs/library/93518/Hung_0603/Hu_0603/HandbookPovertyAnalysisEng.pdf

World Bank (2008). *Measuring Vulnerability* (Last accessed the 2nd of August 2008) http://web.worldbank.org/WBSITE/EXTERNAL/TOPICS/EXTPOVERTY/EXTPA/0,,contentMDK:20238993~menuPK:492141~pagePK:148956~piPK:216618~theSitePK:430367,00.html

Yunus, M. (2006). *Ten indicators to Access Poverty levels*. Grameen Bank website (Last accessed the 2nd of August 2008). http://www.grameen-info.org/index.php?option=com_content&task=view&id=23&Itemid=126

Yunus M (2007). Credit for the poor: poverty as a distant history. *Harvard International Review, Vol.29, no.3*, pp. 20-24.

Zaman, H. (1999). Assessing the poverty and vulnerability impact of microcredit in Bangladesh: case study of BRAC. *Policy Research Working Paper Series 2145*, The World Bank.

Zaman, H. (2004). The Scaling-Up of Microfinance in Bangladesh: Determinants, Impact, and Lessons. *Policy Research Working Paper 3398*, The World Bank.

In: The Other Side of the Coin
Editors: L. Brunori and M. Pines

ISBN: 978-1-62618-726-9

Chapter 5

PSYCHOLOGICAL EFFECTS OF MICROFINANCE: A SYSTEMATIC LITERATURE REVIEW[*]

Giorgia Bonaga[†]
Department of Psychology, University of Bologna, Italy

ABSTRACT

Despite the apparent success and popularity of microfinance, no clear evidence yet exists that microfinance programmes have positive impacts on the borrowers' lives. Furthermore, prior studies have assessed effects of access to credit on traditional economic outcomes for poor borrowers, but effects on psychological well-being have been largely ignored. Therefore, this chapter reports a systematic review of studies published from 1990 to 2011 made by expert researchers on microfinance impact evaluation. I selected and discussed empirical studies focused on psychological issues as empowerment, domestic violence, physical & mental health, and group dynamics. For each investigation area I presented the most frequently used techniques to measure the impact (qualitative and quantitative approaches), research methods and results.

[*] This chapter has significantly benefitted from the information provided by Fabiola Tinessa and suggestions made by Luisa Brunori. The author is grateful to the participants for their contribution on previous version of this work.

[†] Correspondence regarding this chapter may be addressed to giorgia.bonaga@unibo.it; giorgia.bonaga@gmail.com.

Introduction

The literature describes microcredit as a tool for economic development that allows people in poverty and marginalization to have access to financial services.

According to Muhammad Yunus' purpose, founder of the microcredit, this is not just an economic tool, but also, and above all, a means to implement individual and social growth for those who benefit from it.

This experience is based on a representation of man (*homo humanus*), which differs from the one as intended by classical economy (*homo œconomicus*).

The subject, which is generally the primary interest in psychological disciplines, is at the centre of a model of economy that focuses its meaning and its *raison d'être* on the relational system as a source of exchange and generation of resources. The device of microcredit includes the "report" variable, borrowed from the economics discipline, and adds to the psychological discipline the concept of money, intended in terms of value, to exchange wealth, which is both human and practical. In this way, microcredit is constituted as a common ground where dialogue between knowledge and different perspectives is possible.

Disregarding the conceptual and methodological differences between these studies, we will attempt here to construct a meaning line of reasoning through the cross-sectional analysis of the documents produced so far, in order to understand the psycho-social impact of microcredit programs on the life of beneficiaries, their families and the community to which they belong.

Furthermore, this meta-research aims to understand how psychological and social aspects are intertwined with economic ones, often producing sometimes positive and negative outcomes in the individuals' lives. Thanks to this work, it has been possible to classify the studies, around some key topics: (a) "gender empowerment" as referred to political and social participation, decision-making power within the family and in the Community, management of financial resources and monitoring of loans; (b) "domestic violence"; (c) "health and well-being promotion"; (d) "mental health and psychological well-being"; (e) "group dynamics".

Analyzing all the studies as a bloc, a heterogeneous picture comes out, that on the other hand, it lacks of a systematic overview of the phenomenon.

All these contributions highlight the versatile aspect of microcredit, but also the importance of taking into high consideration the social and cultural context in which these programs are implemented.

GENDER EMPOWERMENT

Despite some methodological distinctive features, it is a commonplace belief among the studies on the evaluation of the microcredit's impact that the practice of granting loans preferably to women entails an improvement in the family economic conditions and various other related benefits: i.e. the diversification of livelihoods, the increase in levels of education and the improvement of family members' health conditions. (Todd, 1996; Hulme, Mosley & Khandker, 1996; 1998; Morduch & Haley, 2002; Mosley & Rock, 2004; Zaman, 2004).

However, there is little consensus among these studies, about the possibility that women beneficiaries of these programs can really develop their level of empowerment; as a matter of facts, this is a complex construct measured by indicators and patterns that are always different and inadequate to provide coherent evidences. Some authors believe that microcredit has helped women to increase revenue opportunities, their level of self-confidence and confidence in others, and the ability to overcome cultural asymmetries (Rahman, 1986; Hashemi, Schuler, & Riley, 1996; Pitt & Khandker, 1998; Kabeer, 2001; Pitt, Khandker & Cartwright, 2006). However, other authors believe that loans granted to women are actually managed by their husbands, a situation that could lead to an increase in dependence on them as far as loan installments are concerned, and an exacerbation of pre-existing internal conflicts and incidents of domestic violence (Goetz & SenGupta, 1996; Rahman, 1999; Leach & Sitaram, 2002).

There are several studies that examine the influence of microcredit on female empowerment (Kabeer, 2001) and most of them, thanks to mainly observational and qualitative methods, outline a very positive impact of microcredit on women's lives. Rahman R.I. (1986) found that women taking part in microcredit programs, beside having an income and a consumption rate higher when compared to that of families that do not participate, play an important role in decision-making within the household.

Pitt and Khandker (1995) have measured the impact of microcredit programs on gender identity based on a series of indicators of empowerment. The results showed that, within families involved in microcredit programs, there is more gender equity compared to the other families in which, on the contrary, the women's opinion is taken into little consideration.

Later works (Pitt & Khandker, 1998; Pitt et al., 1999; Pitt, 2000; Pitt et al., 2003) found out that the effects of participation in these programs differ primarily on the base of the gender of the participants. For example, Pitt and

Khandker (1998) argue that the flow of consumption expenditure increases 18 taka for every 100 taka lent to women, but increases only 11 taka for every 100 taka lent to men. Pitt et al. (2003) adopted a completely different approach from the ones previously employed to monitor the identification of microcredit programs' impact, reveal that credit granted to women, improves primarily the quality of life of their children, in terms of greater attention to health and nutrition, while the credit given to men has no statistically significant impact. Furthermore, they pointed out that the credit given to women has a greater chance of influencing their proactive behavior. These results are coherent with the results of the empirical literature. According to them, the mother's control on family resources, even if partial, alters significantly human capital of her children, influencing their life quality to a greater degree.

However, these results do not necessarily imply an increase of the empowerment level within women's lives and within their families. These benefits, in fact, may result from a general improvement of economic conditions and not from the participation in the microcredit program itself.

It is therefore necessary to identify methodological strategies that allow to separate the income effects from the empowerment effect both resulting from the consequent participation in credit programs, thus overcoming what Garikipati (2008) defines the "paradox effect".

Frankenberg and Thomas (2001) suggest that it may be useful to include in the investigation specific and explicit questions on how the decision-making process takes place within the family, arguing that the different models (patterns) of decision-making may result from acquisition of women's power within the family. By employing a special module form used in the second Indonesia Family Life Survey (IFLS2), the authors demonstrate that the combination of qualitative and quantitative approaches enriches the understanding of family dynamics.

Hashemi, Schuler, and Riley (1996) observed a higher level of empowerment among women in the villages where microcredit programs of Grameen Bank and BRAC are employed, compared to women of the villages in which these organizations are not present.

To detect these results they have examined a series of empowerment indicators that included the ability of women to contribute to family income, the freedom of movement (mobility), the ability to make small and large purchases related to their manufacturing activities, the level of involvement in family decision-making and the level of political participation. This study found that access to credit significantly increases contributions to the family income, the probability to own goods, political participation and decision-making in small and large purchases. Access to microcredit also seems to significantly increase the components' value of all the indicators of empowerment, including those which are not found to be significant when are analyzed individually. The results of this study suggest, therefore, that the most appropriate way to increase the empowerment must necessarily pass through the women's ability to contribute to the family income. However, the limitation of these studies is to overlook the potential *bias* arising from the personal characteristics, which are so difficult to observe on an individual, familiar and Community level.

Pitt et al. (2006) suggest adopting an alternative approach which consists in the data collection, through self-reporting, regarding attitudes of and towards women and their degree of autonomy in decision-making. The necessarily subjective nature of the data collected can be corrected thanks to econometric techniques, such as the instrumental variables estimate, which are able to reduce the possible confusing effects due to the systematic variation of the subjective response.

It is important to notice that the results obtained by the majority of previous studies, that have attempted to establish a relationship between participation in credit programs and women's empowerment, were affected by possible bias due to the *endogeneity* of the reasons underlying the decision to participate in the microcredit program, the individual and family variables, and the cultural characteristics of the specific area. The heterogeneity, which could not be observed and therefore a source of possible bias, includes as well the attitudes and characteristics of husbands, wives, other family members, and pre-existing levels of empowerment and autonomy of women. It is possible, for example, that women with a higher level of empowerment are also more likely to join a microcredit program and benefit from it successfully (for a thorough examination see the section of "Domestic violence").

Some studies have also found a negative impact on the empowerment of women. Most of these studies focused on the level of women's control of loans. Goetz and Sengupta (1996), analyzing the index management control of loans, found that the majority of married women have a very limited control, sometimes non-existent control, upon loans (Montgomery, Bhattacharya & Hulme, 1996). This has a negative influence on the repayment process, because when the repayment responsibility is controlled by men and they show a poor capability to face up to it, conflicts light up in the household, thus frustrating all development objectives underlying the practice of microcredit.

Other authors believe that loans to women are in general totally controlled by their husbands. This situation could lead to an increase in the degree of dependence on them and to episodes of internal conflict and violence during the repayment process (Rahman, 1999; Leach & Sitaram, 2002). Dismissing the conceptual and methodological differences between these studies, the results generally suggest, therefore, that although loans to women bring benefits to their families, their beneficial impact on women is somewhat uncertain. The work of Garikipati (2008) tries to unravel some of the reasons behind the *"paradox effect"* by examining separately the impact of microcredit on the beneficiary families and women involved. The sample which was studied comes from two villages in Andhra Pradesh (AP), in India, that are involved in micro-credit program group (SHG). The results seem to confirm the same paradoxical conclusions that characterize the literature on microcredit: even if loans given to women help families to increase income, to diversify means of livelihoods and to reduce vulnerability to family crisis, there has been no increase in the empowerment level of the beneficiaries. The author explores further level of the analysis by examining a combination of credit performance data (such as the use of the loan and the repayment rate) and the direct report of the beneficiaries.

The results suggest that loans granted to women can lead to an improvement in the economic situation of the family. Nevertheless, they do not give them back a co-ownership of family productive activities and cause a further aggravation of the traditional unequal division of resources between wife and husband. The loans given to women are mostly diverted to meet needs of production or consumption of their families; and they are not able to divert income earned through productive activities towards repayment installments. The credit itself will difficulty increase the level of empowerment of women.

To achieve this aim it is necessary to give the credit as part of a broader integrated package that includes other services such as: loans not aimed at the production, savings programs and other related charitable activities that enable women to be the sole owners and managers of goods acquired through loan programs (Berger, 1989; Johnson & Rogaly, 1996; Holvoet, 2005; Mayoux, 2005).

Ashraf, Karlan and Yin (2010), through a randomized and controlled study, have implemented a program that can offer the beneficiaries the ability to manage and control a finance savings fund. This program is not necessarily aimed at increasing the income of the family, but rather to offer a saving device on which only the account holder could exercise control. The product is planned and carried out by the Green Caraga Bank, a rural bank in Philippines.

The customers were randomly selected among the beneficiaries, including in the offer, both independent women and women with limited control on family or marital resources.

The results showed positive impacts, particularly for women who did not have any significant role in the decision-making process. In addition, an important trend was observed among households to invest in durable family goods (*female-oriented*), a progressive improvement of women's ability to self-discipline and the adoption of effective conservation practices of savings.

DOMESTIC VIOLENCE

Recently, there has been a scientific debate about the possibility that microcredit may be qualified as a powerful agent of social change and as an effective means to emerge from poverty (Kabeer, 2001; Roodman & Morduch, 2009;). Some of the researchers' works focus on the specific consequences of women joining the microcredit programs: the improvement of women' social status and the consequent reduction of domestic violence. In the debate on microcredit programs and women's empowerment, marital violence is an issue of critical importance especially in Bangladesh. In this country, there is a rigid patriarchal society and the serious gender inequalities have exacerbated the phenomenon of domestic violence up to a point where this has become almost an accepted and even institutionalized practice (Schuler & Hashemi, 1994; Koenig et al., 2003). In fact, according to the *Demographic and Health Survey*, which collects standardized data from many developing countries, the rates of domestic violence in Bangladesh are among the highest in the world. More than 52% of married women have experienced some form of violence by their husbands during conjugal life.

Microcredit programs, that are particularly present in Bangladesh, where a family out of three is involved, proved to be the ideal ground to monitor and study the phenomenon of domestic violence.

Although several studies have clearly found some positive effects of participation in microcredit groups on domestic violence, the scientific debate recently has been promoted by further studies that have raised serious concerns following the detection of an increased incidence of gender-based violence among women in microcredit programs (Koenig, Ahmed, Hossain & Mazumdar, 2003).

In light of unquestionable results, Schuler et al. (1996) suggest that membership in a microcredit organization is associated with a reduced risk of suffering domestic violence. The study showed a reduction in the levels of violence in two thirds of the families involved in microcredit programs, compared to the families which were not involved. In addition, these positive effects seem to include women who are not members, but who live in villages where microcredit programs are employed.

Koenig et al. (2003) suggest that these beneficial effects may be due to a series of factors. First of all, it could be a consequence of the improvement of economic conditions of the family as a result of the participation of one of the members in microcredit programs. Secondly, the access to credit and the consequent control of a valuable resource such as money could increase women autonomy and raise their status within the family.

Third, the threat of losing the opportunity to receive loans because of the violence could also induce their husbands to become less aggressive (Hashemi, Schuler & Riley, 1996;. Kabeer, 2001). Moreover, the enrichment of the relational support network and the acquisition of a more central place in society, achieved through participation in groups, could reduce domestic violence (Hashemi et al. 1996; Schuler et al., 1996; Schuler, Hashemi, & Badal, 1998).

On the other hand, extensive qualitative studies present more ambiguous results. A study by Schuler et al. (1998) showed that microcredit could exacerbate domestic violence. The violence within families may get worse if the fact of belonging to the group encourages women to challenge traditional gender roles and to maintain control over the resources that are traditionally managed by their husbands. As soon as the husband realizes that the authoritarian control over his wife is compromised because she is a member of a group, the violence increases.

The acquisition of a greater autonomy in economic and social terms would encourage women to gain power within the decision-making by challenging male authority and providing reasons to exacerbate marital and familiar conflict.

Similarly, a study by Rahman A. (1999) has also found that among women who had participated in microcredit groups, over 70% had experienced an increase in violence, and only about 20% had reported a reduction.

However, other studies, including those of Jewkes (2002) and Koenig et al. (2003), have shown the possibility in which the increments of recorded violence can constitute short-term reactions caused by the initial shock that participation to such programs involves, compared to traditional gender norms. These negative effects, however, may decrease in the long term as a result of the increase in the level of women empowerment. In a long-term, the group membership tends to be a protective factor from gender-based violence (World Bank, 2009).

The study of Ahmed (2005), from the Research and Assessment of BRAC Centre confirms this hypothesis. The author used a subset of cross-cultural data collected in 1999 including 60 studies of BRAC-ICDDR.B conducted in the villages of Matlab, in Bangladesh, to compare women who participated in BRAC programs with those who did not. The highest level of domestic violence, reported in the early stages of participation in BRAC, decreases in the course of time. The author attributes this result to the participation of women in training programs which are planned to provide members with financial and health information.

On the basis of these contradictory evidences, the development of a conclusive hypothesis about the possibility that microcredit could influence domestic violence remains therefore mainly unsolved.

The Selection Bias

It is important to highlight that most of the studies that have examined the microcredit group membership and its effects on women, have been based largely on a cross-sectional sample. In this way, the question of the selection bias was inadequately treated. The results illustrated above can therefore be misleading (Steele, Amin & Naved, 2001).

In facts, it is necessary to considerate that the default selection (self selection) of women in microcredit groups may already make them part of a group more naturally empowered and therefore resistant to domestic violence.

On the other hand, studies by Schuler et al. (1996) suggest that women belonging to microcredit groups may already be more vulnerable to domestic violence, as they have high levels of empowerment and they are inclined to challenge the gender rules and to cause constant conjugal tensions.

While factors such as high levels of empowerment and of education appear to be protective factors against domestic violence, the cross-cultural research, as observed by Jewkes (2002), suggests that within the societies with a patriarchal dominant ideology, domestic violence tends to be more frequent. The social and institutional structures contribute to make women, with more liberal ideas and opinions, victims of violence committed by their husbands or by other male members of the community. These risks remain until the level of women's empowerment does not reach a high enough level so to constitute the predominant protective factor.

Another possible selection *bias* comes from the tangible possibility that women, who participate in a microcredit program, may have the socio-economic characteristics that make them innately more vulnerable to domestic violence. As it has been demonstrated, the poverty condition is one of the features closely related to high levels of domestic violence (Heise, 1998; Ellsberg et al., 1999; Jewkes, 2002) and microcredit programs are mainly directed to the poorest rural population[1], coming from the lowest socio-economic groups.

As it is widely supported by the scientific literature, if the poor women were more likely to experience domestic violence than non-poor women, then the members of the microcredit group would belong to a category inherently more vulnerable to violence. In conclusion, it is not possible to argue that a higher level of violence between members of microcredit can be attributed unequivocally to the effects of the program (Steele, Amin & Naved 2001).

Some disagreement is still present in the literature on the nature of the connection between poverty and domestic violence. Some studies have shown that this correlation becomes insignificant when there are protective factors such as an average level of education and quality life. (Diop-Sidibe, 2001).

Hadi (2000), who is interested in investigating the phenomenon of violence with an experimental method, employed semi-structured interviews to collect information on socio-demographic characteristics, and more in-depth individual interviews which focused on the topic of exposure to sexual violence, as well as on the nature of the relationship with the partner.

The findings of the research are not supported by statistical significance, but by trend values. The socio-demographic characteristics that have been examined suggest that the age, the enrolment level, and the socio-economical status are related to episodes of abuse. In particular, the occurrence of violence decreases in older couples and it is inversely proportional to the woman level of education. The research results show also that the risk of abuses is higher among the low-income families. Furthermore, the financial contribution to the family expenses reduces the probability of being sexually abused.

Hadi confirms this hypothesis in his later work (2005) by identifying age, enrolment of education, standard of living and "late" marriage as the main

[1] The significant correlation between poverty and domestic violence is primarily explained/justified by an influential theory that suggests that families living in poverty have higher levels of stress and have fewer resources to fight than the non-poor families, and that stress mediates the relationship between poverty and domestic violence, making poor women more likely to suffer from domestic violence (Jewkes, 2002; Kishor & Johnson, 2006).

determinants involved in incidents of psychological and physical violence against women.

The results indicate that, although neither the causes that lead a man to be violent, nor the mechanisms by which participation in credit programs change these behaviors are fully known. The probabilities that a woman will suffer from an abuse increases if she is young, illiterate and poor, and decreases if she belongs to a group of microcredit and has started a profitable business.

The hypothesis that the author formulates to explain the results of this study is that the beneficiaries of micro-credit will help to reduce the poverty-induced stress experienced by their husbands thanks to the revenues of their activities, or the amount of the loan received (Schuler et al., 1998). Consequently, the possibility for these women to negotiate the family decisions with their husband and to modify the couple relationships increases. In addition, it can be argued that being able to contribute financially to the family income may encourage women victims of violence to take a more active role within the family.

However, according to Kishor and Johnston (2006), the inconsistency of the effects of the family socio-economic status on domestic violence may depend on the variability of the existing definitions of the concept of poverty, wealth and domestic violence.

Poverty, which currently seems to be the element most strongly related to the phenomena of violence against women, also appears to be linked to a number of other specific factors which are also associated to the risk of domestic violence. As Heise's conceptual framework shows (1998), the factors that determine the risk of domestic violence may be individual, relational, familiar, social and cultural. (Heise, 1998; Naved & Persson, 2005).

Among the individual factors, there are episodes of previous exposure to personal and intergenerational violence, to conflict within the marital relationship and to the dynamics of unequal power. On the other hand, among familiar, social and cultural factors there are the family and community structure that emphasizes on male progeny and on social tolerance towards violence against women. The overall evidence may suggest that poverty can have strong influences on each one of these aspects, which in turn, can potentially constitute risk factors related to domestic violence.

In conclusion, in order to obtain rigorous evidence, it is necessary to plan research models that take into high consideration the problem of selection bias; this research should be able to encompass the individual, family and cultural variables, as well as the socio-economic factors related to domestic violence in populations at risk.

The most recent *matched case-control studies* are to be included in this perspective. Bajracharya and Amin (2010) extracted from the Bangladesh Demographic Health Survey of 2007, a sample of married women (N = 4,195), using the Propensity Score Matching (PSM) method to explore the selection *bias* compared in relation to the correlation between the participation in microcredit groups and the increase in domestic violence. The results suggest that the positive correlation found in earlier studies (Schuler et al. 1998) between the membership and the violence does not occur when the analysis uses an appropriate comparison group, generated thanks to the PSM.

On the one hand, these results are at odds with the assumption that microcredit could exacerbate domestic violence as a consequence of the challenge put out by women to traditional gender norms. On the other hand, they do not confirm the results (Schuler et al., 1996; Koenig et al., 2003) which postulate the existence of positive effects of membership on domestic violence. When the distinctive factors and *bias* related to selection are equally and adequately distributed among the members and non-members (control group and experimental group), the participation to microcredit program does not seem to have a great influence on domestic violence.

For what concerns the empowerment's dimension, the results that stand out are coherent with the idea that the women's participation in microcredit programs helps to increase their empowerment. The credit programs help women to play a more important role in family decision-making process, to have A greater access to financial and economic resources, to expand their social networks, to increase their bargaining power towards their husbands and to have greater freedom of movement. They also tend to improve the quality of marital communication in general and regarding the family planning and parenting concerns. The effects of male control of credit on the empowerment of women were generally negative. The presence of males in microcredit programs had, in fact, a negative effect on the results measured on the general empowerment of the selected families, in particular on the control of resources by women, on finance, on the freedom of movement, the development of social networks and decisions of fertility and parenthood.

Health and Well-being Promotion

Micro-credit is one of the interventions that can significantly contribute to enhance women health. The improvement of the socio-economic conditions also increases the chances of access to valuable information about health.

According to Mohindra, Haddad and Narayana (2008), there are 4 ways, which can take from participation in microcredit programs to the promotion of well-being: the economic way, the social way, the psycho-social way and the political way. The improvement of the economic conditions leads to the increased access to community resources and public goods or services. The construction of a social support network helps to increase the pressure on social and cultural rules that influence health behaviors; an enhanced level of self-esteem and self-awareness gives to women the opportunity to be actively engaged in the pursuit of individual and family well-being. In the end, a higher degree of women development in economical, psychological and social terms may result in a stronger political and decisional power, which could influence women's right to access to public resources.

The studies produced so far have provided solid evidences relating the mothers' participation in the microcredit and the consequent improvement of mother / child health in terms of conscious use of contraceptive methods, knowledge of appropriate care in the pre and post natal period, control stages of growth and development of the child. In addition, there have been positive outcomes in other dimensions that affect the woman health such as the personal nutritional status and the frequency of access to hospital services.

Nevertheless, all the studies suffer from the lack of a theoretical framework. The available evidences derive from cross-sectional studies and are restricted to their applicative field; this precludes the possibility of generalizing the results and to identify a causal connection between participation in microcredit programs and the health promotion. Most of the studies on this topic have examined the Grameen Bank and other popular programs in Bangladesh, providing little information about micro-credit programs in other regions of the world. The analysis of this association would require the application of more rigorous studies that will avoid influencing the results.

It is highly likely that microcredit is neither a panacea to alleviate poverty, nor it can possibly affect all aspects of health. Yet, it can play a crucial role in promoting the health of women and their families, bringing about a consequent improvement of individual and family well-being. The following studies confirm that, through an intervention carried out on the individual, or on the group, it is possible to produce changes and improvements to the whole community, creating a virtuous circle that brings benefits to the whole system in terms of widespread diffusion of prevention measures and health promotion.

Nanda (1999) analyzed some data from a sample of 1798 households in the Rural Bangladesh, collected from 87 districts covered by the financial services of the Grameen Bank and the *Bangladesh Rural Advance Committee* (BRAC) in order to detect whether participation in microcredit programs could have a significant effect on family access to health services. The results confirm this hypothesis and highlight the efficiency of these credit programs, which, along with other financial services, also develop actions to promote health in order to increase the decision-making power of women within the family and the Community.

Doocy et al. (2005) focus on evaluating the nutritional status of a group of farmers in Ethiopia during a period of drought and food shortage, cross-checking the differences between new and old customers of wisdom *Microfinance Institution* and a Community of control with no microcredit programs. This cross-sectional study has been conducted on three groups of 819 families. Based on an overall assessment on the family conditions of malnutrition, the results highlight some important differences between the examined groups. The women who have been in long time microcredit programs showed better health and less need to use food aids.

Since no significant differences have been noticed within and between groups, in relation to the use of appropriate coping strategies, better health conditions experienced by some individuals may not be attributed to the different individual skills when dealing with situations of crisis.

A study carried out in the Dominican Republic by Dohn et al. (2004) evaluated the impact of different methodologies of health promotion on three separate distinct communities.

In one community only a program of health promotion has been carried out, in another one a microcredit program and in the third both of them. The authors' starting hypothesis, based on 11 indicators of well-being adopted for the valuation, claimed to record better outcomes within the community that had benefited from both interventions and less important outcomes in the communities that had benefited only from the microcredit program.

The results showed an improvement in all three communities. However, in communities where there were both financial aid and interventions for health promotion, there have been major increases in indicators of well-being compared to the communities in which only the single intervention was implemented.

The study of Mohindra et al. (2008) analyzes the correlations between female participation in a microcredit program in Kerala, based on the Self Help Groups (SHG), and the effectiveness of the health promotion intervention for women conveyed by the program. This cross-sectional study is based on data provided by a special survey carried out in 2003 by a

Panchayat (local self-governments); this study has allowed to collect detailed information on the individual characteristics of women, on their behavior in matter of health, (e.g. self-exclusion from health care, level of exposure to health risks, decision-making power in the family) and their actual conditions of psychophysical well-being (by self report). The study sample included 928 young women of low socio-economic status.

The results show that, among families with a beneficiary of microcredit programs, the probability of being excluded from health systems is significantly lower (especially among those who have been members for more than two years) than recent members (less than two years).

Families in which there are no beneficiaries of microcredit programs, however, are more likely to be excluded from the health care system. Furthermore, the results show that those who have been members of SHG for a longer time, are less likely to experiment forms of physical and emotional stress than non-members. No correlation between the participation in the SHG and the level of overall exposure to health risks, has been identified.

The scientific literature unanimously agrees in attributing to microcredit programs an important role in the prevention of sexually transmitted infectious diseases in developing countries.

In connection to this, recent events have highlighted the growing interest of the research to identify in the microfinance the elective strategy for the reduction of HIV risk (Stratford et al., 2008).

The growing popularity of the studies that have analyzed the effects of the integration of HIV/AIDS prevention programs into microfinance programs may be due, first, to the belief that microfinance could be a promising strategy to mitigate the adverse/negative economic impact on all those who are affected by it (Barnes, 2003; 2005; Parker, 2000); secondly, the need to investigate the issue of sustainability and the actual ability to refund loans of customers who come from developing countries where there is a higher risk of contracting HIV/AIDS (Mayoux, 2001; Bundred, 2006; Gommans, 2006).

To emphasize the economic empowerment of women seems to be the most effective and urgent prevention strategy within the struggle for the reduction of the risk of contracting HIV/AIDS.

The results of the literature indicates that women in disadvantageous economic conditions or economically dependent are more likely to adopt high-risk behaviours in terms of infectious diseases transmission, because they are less capable to negotiate safe sex with their partners, they are less likely to stand up against a violent intercourse (which also increases the risk of contracting HIV), and they are more likely to offer sexual performances in exchange for material goods (Exner et al., 2003; Hallman, 2004).

In addition, some studies have found that many women begin to prostitute themselves because they are forced, then they are trapped in for economic reasons (Manopaiboon et al., 2003; Minh Tan et al., 2004). Well-known studies show that the economic independence of women is an important protective factor that enables them to negotiate safe sex (Grieg & Koopman, 2003; Hallman, 2004). Thus, the way that microcredit programs are able to provide women with alternative sources of income and to promote their economic emancipation, can also promote the adoption of behaviors that prevent the risk of contracting the virus.

There are very few economic studies on integrated programs of microcredit and prevention of HIV, which have been tested on a national or international level. Between September 2001 and March 2005, Hargreaves, Pronyk and Kim (2006) conducted the study IMAGE "*With Microfinance for AIDS and Gender Equity*" in rural Limpopo in South Africa. They used a cluster randomized experimental framework. The hypothesis they evaluated suggested that the combination of the participation in a program for poverty reduction and in training on HIV prevention and gender rights, may improve the economic and social well-being of women, reducing significantly the domestic violence.

The evaluation of results, based on the presence of domestic violence episodes and the analysis of 9 indicators of the level of women empowerment, shows that after two years the risk of physical violence or sexual abuse suffered in the previous year was reduced by more than half. In addition, improvements were observed in respect to all nine indicators of empowerment: women have proved more able to negotiate the use of contraceptive practices with partners, to dissociate themselves from violent relationships and to make other women in the community aware of these subjects.

All the studies presented about health and well-being dimension, even though are originated from different contexts of applications, have always noticed a positive correlation between the participation in microcredit programs and an improvement in health and well-being of those who took part in it. These data demonstrate the importance of the impact of microcredit on a social level and the value of self-employment, which gives the person a greater opportunity to influence their own destiny with consequent significant improvements, not only for themselves but also for their families in terms of food and health safety.

Mental Health and Psychological Well-being

According to the *Le Rapport sur la santé dans le Monde* of 2001 by WHO, there is a relationship between poverty and mental health. Poverty can be a motivating factor or a risk factor for depression, suicide, abuse of alcohol and illegal drugs. In general, for other diseases, poverty contributes to the deterioration of the individual's living conditions.

There is no direct evidence that the reduction of poverty can result in a benefit to the mental health of a population, but on the contrary it is proved that mental disease has a significant role in perpetuating the poverty conditions.

An extensive scientific literature has shown that emotional stress caused by poverty and precarious economic conditions, may lead to the development and / or maintenance of common mental disorders such as anxiety and depression (Bruce, Takeuchi & Leaf, 1991; Rodgers, 1991; Weich & Lewis, 1998). It is also known that physical illness can also be a consequence of emotional stress, since psychological well-being is constituted as a protective factor against premature mortality and disease (Stewart-Brown, 1998). The disadvantaged condition of women in developing countries society increases their chances of experiencing stressful life situations, which can in turn trigger or exacerbate episodes of mental illness (Patel et al., 1999; Sherrill et al., 1997).

In a multicentric study, conducted by WHO on psychological problems in general health care, women were found to be 1.6 times more likely to suffer from depression and anxiety disorder, or panic disorder with agoraphobia than men (Gater et al., 1998). This difference appears to result from a combination of factors related to the methods used to cope with stress, to biological components and to the social context of belonging (Paykel, 1991).

Khatun, Wadud, Bhuiya, and Chowdhury (1998), in planning a study which focused on developing a scale of indicators for measuring the psychological well-being of women in rural communities, have recognized the importance of the inclusion of the so-called "intangible" goods in the evaluation of individuals and communities' quality of life.

Development programs that aim to improve the individuals' "tangible" economic dimension, generally disregard the impact of subjective factors involved in the discrepancy between initial expectations and achievements, as well as the impact that anxieties and tensions, which derive from newly adopted non-traditional roles by women, can have on the their emotional and physical well-being.

A following study by Chowdhury and Bhuiya (2001) analyzes the episodes of emotional stress experienced by poor women in rural areas involved in the programs of BRAC for credit-based income-generating activities, in the region of Matlab, in Bangladesh.

The authors compared a group of women beneficiaries of microcredit programs with a group of women not beneficiaries and members of similar socioeconomic status.

Multivariate analysis revealed that BRAC interventions in Matlab are associated with a significant and positive increase in the economic well-being (Husain et al., 1996); however, no discernible difference relative to the higher prevalence of emotional distress among poorest women was revealed.

The results also indicate that, in the early stage of the program implementation, microcredit does not seem to positively influence the emotional and psychological well-being of the recipients. Indeed, it could be argued that the involvement in productive activities initially cause a greater emotional stress, especially if some factors are simultaneously considered as predictors of psychological distress: a family atmosphere of conflict, a large number of children, a precarious state of physical health and disputes with neighbors, often caused by disputes over generational transfer of land ownership (Momen, Bhuiya & Chowdhury, 1995).

As BRAC interventions in Matlab have been activated in recent times (at the time of the survey the maximum membership length was 22 months), we should assume that this period cannot be considered sufficient to influence the lives of the poor, particularly on their emotional well-being.

This hypothesis is strengthened by the fact that, in the selected sample, it was found a high prevalence of depression symptoms, which were already present before the participation in microcredit programs.

Almost half of the people interviewed (mostly belonging to the experimental group of BRAC) was characterized by the adoption of a fatalistic attitude and resignation in coping with stressful situations in daily life and showed a general lack of confidence in personal coping capabilities in situations of crisis.

Some authors focused on the study of the negative psychological factors that seem to be involved in the participation in the microcredit program. One of these is the stress caused by the pressure of the peer group used in several methods (joint liability) as a substitute for the collateral on the systematic collection of the loan. Rahman A. (1999) points out that many beneficiaries are able to support a pattern of regular repayment through a process of loan recycling that significantly increases the debt of individual families thus exacerbating the frustration and tension within the family.

It should be noted also, that women recipients of micro-credit programs must challenge the existing gender socio-cultural norms in order to manage an independent economic activity and to achieve the objectives underlying the practice of the loan.

The time they dedicate to the production of income-generating as well as organizational activities (team meetings, training courses, etc.), takes time away from marital and parental obligations, and can compromise the balance of family.

Therefore, it is not correct to assume that to an increase in the socio-economic well-being, necessarily corresponds an improvement in the psycho-emotional well-being. The psycho-emotional well-being is, in fact, a subjective state that reflects the general situation of the individual: at the social, physical and material level.

Generally development interventions focus mainly on the improvement of the material conditions of life (tangible) of program beneficiaries such as increased income through productive investments, retaining and/or accumulating assets that allow to cope with crisis situations, investing in children's education and family health care (Hulme, 2000).

The improvement of the subjective factors that contribute to maintaining a high quality of life in terms of psychological well-being is rarely evaluated. Many critics argue that organizations that promote the development which focus on women as a priority group have failed to recognize their specific vulnerability to common mental disorders (Patel et al., 1999).

Patel and Kleinman (2003) were commissioned by the World Health Organization (WHO) a review of eleven studies from six countries in Africa, Asia, and Latin America, with the aim of analyzing the theoretical processes underlying the correlation between mental illness and poverty to identify the most appropriate prevention plans.

The results indicate a high prevalence of depressive and anxiety disorders, according to the ICD-10 classification[2]. Ten out of eleven studies reviewed showed a significant relationship between the incidence of mental illness and indicators of poverty. In light of the results obtained, the authors inserted the device of microcredit among the strategic proposals of primary and secondary prevention.

---

[2] Tenth Revision of the International Statistical Classification of Diseases and Related Health Problems

More recently Patel et al. (2010) conducted a systematic review of the epidemiological literature interested in analyzing the relationship between poverty and mental disorders. Among the 115 studies reviewed, the bivariate analysis identified in 79% of them a prevalence of positive associations between some indicators of poverty and the prevalence rate of common mental disorders, no significant correlation in 19% of them and in 8% the presence of negative associations.

However, a closer examination of the specific dimensions of poverty reveals a more complex picture, where there are substantial differences between these dimensions. While variables such as lack of education, food insecurity, poor quality housing, low socioeconomic status and financial tensions are relatively consistent and strong association with common mental disorders, other factors such as income, employment and the rate of consumption show weaker associations. These variations can be explained taking into account the different methodological measurements and factors specific to the target population.

For what concerns mental health and psychological well-being dimension, the available data are not sufficient to assert that the microcredit can be established as a the therapeutic tool in the fight against the development of mental disorders related to poverty. However, based on the Patel and Kleinman conclusions and on others authors' findings, as mentioned above, microcredit can be considered as an effective strategy.

Programs that invest in the education and microcredit can have the unexpected effect of reducing the risk of mental disorder. In this sense, microcredit probably cannot affect the decrease in the number of people suffering from mental illness, but it may perhaps prevent a greatest number of people from being affected by it.

Group Dynamics

The prolific literature dedicated to this subject presents many definitions of the word "group", most of them very interesting, but at the same time, very oversimplified. Whatever the correct definition would be, we know for certain that the group is a "place" within which some dynamics occur, that influence the behavior of all its members.

The research presented below demonstrates that, in the planning of microcredit programs, it is essential to take into account these dynamics in order to ensure the success of the project.

The Grameen model, the most popular micro-credit project in the world, is based on the system of the *solidarity group*. This method is currently used in more than 43 countries and it is based on the creation of a mutual aid group that supports each beneficiary. The loan is provided by the bank only if the applicant is part of a group of at least five people.

There are no legal instruments which regulate the relations between the Grameen Bank and its members; the whole system is based on trust. To integrate the loan, Grameen Bank requires regular members to save a small amount of money that will create an emergency fund for the members and for the group. These funds are used to contain potential contingent debt insolvencies.

The *solidarity groups* are generally very small, formed by a maximum of 5 members; they constitute the ideal size to provide the group with the highest level of shared responsibility discouraging opportunistic behavior, and to prevent the collapse of the group because of the unreliability of one of its members.

There are other methods of credit-based group representing variants of the *solidarity group*: they eliminate the problem of adverse selection and moral hazard as they depend on a cross-collateralization guarantee system by which each member of the group guarantees the repayment of other members. These methods, used by Villages Banking, Self Help Groups and, in a massive way, *joint liability groups*, are given special attention by the subject studies, since, if on the one hand, the fear of damaging their reputation acts as a regulatory mechanism of the loan, on the other hand it creates inconvenience to beneficiaries hindering the development process.

This methodology is often associated with an improvement in repayment rates and lower transaction costs, since the loan between peers provides incentives to self-monitor each other and to enforce each other's reimbursement processes. By creating a group of customers linked to each other in the loan, the lender can take advantage of the local information to improve the selection, monitoring and enforcement of the credit mechanism. Thanks to the group responsibility, customers are encouraged to select other clients so that only trustworthy people could qualify for the program. In addition, customers will ensure that loans are properly invested in profitable companies. Finally, the performance tends to improve as customers are faced with peer pressure, as well as legal, to repay their loans.

In recent years, some microfinance institutions, such as the *Association for Social Advancement* (ASA) in Bangladesh or the Bank Rakyat in Indonesia (BRI), have reported a rapid expansion growth thanks to individual responsibility loans. Others, like BancoSol in Bolivia, have converted a large portion of the loan portfolio of groups of shared responsibility in groups of loan to individual responsibility. Even the Grameen Bank has recently (1998-2000) relaxed the clause, which regulates the responsibilities of group in the Grameen II program by allowing defaulters to renegotiate their loans without working on the group pressure. Many of these groups (for example, ASA) have implemented this change, while assuring the presence of the group. So, while the responsibility is individual, group process helps lenders to reduce transaction costs, while maintaining the benefits of sharing of the loan as the selection and monitoring of peers. The shift to individual responsibility has not only characterized the history of Grameen Bank and a few other big MFI, but also the story of many donors from around the world.

This shift from group responsibility to individual liability has accelerated the microfinance community learning process on issues related to the responsibilities of the group.

First, customers do not like the tension caused by the shared responsibility: the excessive tension among members, in fact, is not only responsible for voluntary interruptions, but, worse, it can also harm impair social capital among members, which is particularly important in ensuring the consistency of the safety networks. Second, the opportunism of some members can infect the good customers resulting in an increase in the default rate. In other words, a customer cannot repay the loan because they know that someone else will pay for them, relying on the institution's indifference.

Third, the group liability is more expensive for good customers who are often required to repay the loans of their peers. This can lead to an increase of drop out and an increase in the difficulty in attracting new customers.

Moreover, the heterogeneity of lending can cause tension within the group so that clients with smaller loans may be reluctant to act as a guarantor for those with larger loans. In conclusion, while the reimbursement rate may improve in terms of shared responsibility, the number of customers is likely to decrease, so it is still unclear whether group liability improves the overall profitability of the MFI and facilitates the access of the poor to financial market.

Although this is an issue of fundamental importance, the empirical research on the group responsibilities *versus* individual liability did not produce clear evidence to help determine the values of the two different methodologies, for policymakers and institutions.

This question has remained unanswered, since the MFI generally choose a type depending on the context in which they operate; the majority of micro lenders, in fact, tends to use only one type of loan and it is therefore difficult to identify the impact of different methodology of agreements, through a cross-sectional study in the same context.

In some cases, the mechanism of shared responsibility implies that the beneficiaries indicate a co-guarantor, usually a family member or a friend, to engage in a sharing of responsibility for the entire process of loan repayment.

The application of the mechanism of this informal control may entail an excessive pressure on the beneficiary, thus risking to expose him to the social stigma or to some form of collective punishment (Besley & Coate, 1995), or in extreme cases, to tragic results as the suicide of the beneficiaries. The correlation between social stigma and suicide risk has been widely documented in other disciplines.

Bresley (1995), for example, has observed this phenomenon among the members of a microcredit program in Japan which provided a system of joint liability with a co-guarantor. Chen, Choi and Sawada (2010) attempt an analysis of how a loan could result, in some occasions, in an increase in the suicide rate among borrowers bound by a contract to a third party as guarantor. The results of a survey of 305 participants (52 self-employed and 243 employed) reveal that 46.2% of self-employed (n 24 of 52) made a suicide attempt because of multiple debts and / or because involved in a contract of joint liability, compared to 14.4% among employed persons (n 39 of 243). In addition, approximately one third of suicides committed by the self-employed (n 17 of 52) was due to problems of co-guarantee, as compared to 3.6 in suicides among employed persons (n 9 of 253), due to the same problem.

The literature is focused almost exclusively on the comparison of the repayment performance between that of shared responsibility in group and individual. Ghatak and Guinnane (1999) suggest that group liability can help institutions to increase the reimbursement rate through four channels: (i) ensuring the level of risk default by the beneficiaries (adverse selection), (ii) ensuring that the loans are used correctly (*ex-ante* /before the event of moral hazard), (iii) ensuring that beneficiaries tell the truth in the case of non-compliance (monitoring), (iv) encouraging the payment if a borrower is unwilling reluctant to repay/refund the loan (voluntary default).

Other studies suggest that group liability may instead jeopardize the repayment of individuals. For example, Besley and Coate (1995) point out that the beneficiaries would refund the loan in situation of individual responsibility, but maybe they would not do this in a situation of group responsibility. There may happen, in fact, that reliable members realize that they cannot cope as a group with others persons' insolvencies of others and then, on the basis of the existing rules, cannot apply to further loans at a later stage. In this case, even the members who are able to repay may decide to become non-compliant since the incentive of future claims has lost its meaning.

Madajewicz (2005) argues that the responsibility of the group is suitable only for very poor clients. In his model, in fact, all loans are substantial (considerable amount) as the situation of group responsibility encourages members to take a higher risk, and to realize riskier projects. The richest customers prefer to be part of an individual responsibility methodology.

To confirm this hypothesis, the MFI tends to use a type of individual contracts with customers that have proven to be more successful in the development process.

In an attempt to make a contribution to the debate, Ginè, and Karlan (2007) conducted an experiment at the Green Bank of Caraga in the Philippines. The authors have assigned random half of the 169 branches existing credit, originally based on the model *joint liability group*, in centres based on the methodology individual (treatment group), preserving in the other half the methodology liability group (control group). Through this conversion, the authors were able to value the superiority in terms of efficacy and overcoming information asymmetries of either method.

The results indicated that the conversion of existing centers in a methodology for individual type did not affect the reimbursement rate and led to a growth of the number of members by facilitating the recruitment of new customers. In addition, it was found that individual responsibility has resulted in a reduction of the monitoring in relation to repayment performances, not affecting default rate.

Despite undeniably good results related to microfinance programs, the literature has paid particular attention to the evaluation of the quality of self-entrepreneurial projects, neglecting the method by which human resources are to be assembled to support such projects. Within the methodology of group responsibility, what are the mechanisms that facilitate the performance and exploit the potential of social capital to ensure a successful outcome of the process of individual and community development?

Woolcok (1999) analyzes various cases of the failure of some microfinance programs based on the methodology group, in order to understand their mode of operation. He considers five cases of group approaches to microfinance coming from a larger retrospective and comparative study on organizational problems in microfinance programs, and which failed at different levels. Each of these cases has been chosen to show

how the non-payment of the loan is both cause and effect of the collapse of the strategic joints of the MFI organizational structure.

In this sense, to measure the performance of microfinance programs only just on the basis of the rate of return and financial sustainability is highly reductive, because, often, low rates of return are caused by factors such as the structural weakness of the organization and the inability to develop human resources.

An interesting study by Anthony (2005) sought to analyze the dynamics of collaboration and cooperation developed within groups of microcredit borrowers. These groups are considered to be an ideal setting to study these phenomena, as the members who belong to have the task of ensuring the "availability of credit" to each other which becomes a public good, through the unanimous adherence compliance to rules requiring the return of the loan within an agreed timeframe.

Within the groups of credit, there are some dynamics, generated by the conditions of interdependence of individuals who participate such as: *externality*[3], self-management, monitoring, collective responsibility and regularity of meetings which help to strengthen the sense of belonging and identification of the members of the group itself.

Anthony refers to three different theories from group studies in order to understand the mechanisms of identity of the group in this context. According to the *Social Identity Theory* (Tajfel, 1981), individuals within a group tend to cooperate more if they feel part of it, in other words, the level of cooperation among the members is strongly associated with the intensity of their identification with the group. According to the theory of Tajfel, groups in which members have powerful feelings of membership there will be higher levels of adherence to group norms (compliance) and increased production of the collective good.

According to the *Logic of collective action* by Olson (1965), the collective action is difficult to be produced because, although the benefits are shared, the costs are sustained individually, so individuals rationally choose not to cooperate. According to Olson, the collective actions for success need incentives, such as rewards or punishments, which are able to regulate the conduct of compliance or non-compliance of individuals.

Other authors argue and demonstrate that the penalties increased levels of social control and compliance within the group. Based on this hypothesis, the

---

Externalities occur when the unconscious action of a person causes positive or negative impact in the personal sphere of other persons.

groups ruled by punitive sanctions should produce a greater collective good and a higher level of *compliance*.

A third school focuses on the ways in which social relations among members of a group influence cooperative behaviors. The reciprocity mechanism, involved in the production of the collective good, strengthens the cooperation between the members, because it generates high levels of trust and engagement between the partners involved. The paradigm of interest leads to the formulation of the third hypothesis: the groups in which members are involved in reciprocal relationships will produce a greater collective good and a higher level of compliance.

The groups of borrowers considered in this study are included in the program of *Working Capital* loans, a large non-profit organization for the development of the community.

Through a telephone survey, carried out on a representative sample, it was possible to collect data on individual borrowers and groups.

This analysis showed that the strength of the group, the presence of sanctions and reciprocal relationships are all variables associated with a high number of requests for loans within the group; this indicates that both the identification with the group and the personal interests are closely related to the production of the common good. The level of compliance found in groups, do not seem to be influenced by the strength of the group and the presence of disciplinary sanctions, but groups with a high "*commonality*" are more likely to comply with the rules of the group and therefore less likely to be in default.

In conclusion, only the reciprocity between members is significantly associated with a lower default rate and more likely to last. Although the production of a collective good and a high level of *compliance*, even though they are mechanisms that facilitate initial cooperation within the group, they are not responsible for the survival of the group over time.

Finally, the results presented relatively to the dynamic group dimension, have shown that groups can have a decisive effect in the processes of individual and collective development: emerging from poverty and promoting the goals achievement that individuals could not conquer on their own.

Therefore, the effect of social support, which is perceived in a cohesive group, could help increase the perception of the sense of security and reduce the sense of helplessness in the individual, encouraging him to deconstruct existing hierarchies of power and reduce inequalities.

According to this perspective, the groups play a particularly important role in the management and creation of devices that focus on increasing financial stability through micro-credit programs in the poorest communities.

So, in the interest of enhancing the contribution of the financial services offered by microfinance institutions in the process of community development, it is necessary to understand the role of groups, their effects, and the relationship between individuals and groups, particularly towards the community.

Collective activities, community-based and participatory, are intended to reflect and meet more successfully the needs of the communities involved to ensure the implementation of more sustainable development activities.

This approach is based on the belief that a delegation of powers and responsibilities to rural communities enable them to become an effective means of development for the Community itself (Mansuri & Rao, 2004).

It includes the idea of promoting and supporting local institutions as vehicles for development, particularly when they are involved in this process through external agencies (institutions). The collective action thus promotes ownership of development initiatives through the participation of the entire community, which becomes a necessary tool to influence political decisions, and gain the satisfaction of basic needs (Seyfang, 2003).

As a result, groups can play an important role in increasing both the economic and political power of poor communities, through the resolution of market failures, as well as the access of the poor to financial markets, managing common resources in a better way and implementing income-generating activities. (Stewart, 2005).

Heyer et al. (2002) argue that groups are crucial to individual and collective good because they are able to change self-awareness, self-esteem, identity, ideology and the sense of justice in the individual.

CONCLUSION

The wide range of contributions collected in this meta-research confirms the multidimensional nature of the microcredit. This phenomenon is influenced by tangible aspects, but also by social and relational ones.

Such complexity cannot be understood by determining dichotomously the good / bad quality of the practice, because that depends from a big quantity of variables.

In fact, it is obvious that not all borrowers can benefit in the same way from the intervention of microcredit; the outcome often depends on the local economy, their entrepreneurial skills and the extent to which the sources of income are diversified. However, there are many evidences that point out the fundamental contribution of microcredit, in positively influencing gender relations and encouraging women, through access to credit, to take a greater role in decision-making in their family and social life.

Moreover, the debate on the impact of microcredit is incomplete without a reference to the wider non-financial assistance package that comes with credit (Microfinance Plus). The non-financial services offered by MFI vary significantly and typically include: training, targeted support to business development and social interventions aimed at promoting the right to education and health. It seems that, in the developing countries, social interventions combined with financial services are able to increase the profits of self-employment by 175%.

Another aspect to be considered, is related to many "decisive and resolving" expectations that micro-credit has excited since its foundation. Certainly, it has set the hope on more human social relationships: relationships that we all desperately need to live and survive, but microfinance is not a panacea and it is clearly not able to eliminate all poverty in every country in the world. Also, if it is not properly monitored, the device can be a trap for customers who do not use loans productively and in danger of falling into the hyper-debt.

Therefore, the role of microfinance should be reinforced through further innovations that take account of these variables and of these risks. Its potential could be better exploited by recognizing and adopting the suggestions from impact evaluation studies in a more accurate and rigorous way.

References

Ahmed, S., Chowdhury, M., & Bhuiya, A. (2001). Micro-credit and emotional well-being: Experience of poor rural women from Matlab, Bangladesh. *World Development, 29:11,* pp. 1957-1966.

Ahmed, S. M. (2005). Intimate partner violence against women: Experiences from a woman-focused development programme in Matlab, Bangladesh. *Journal of Health, Population and Nutrition, 23,* pp. 95-101.

Anthony, D. (2005). Cooperation in Microcredit Borrowing Groups: Identity, Sanctions, and Reciprocity in the Production of Collective Goods. *American Sociological Review, June 70*, pp. 496-515.

Ashraf, N., Karlan, D., & Yin, W. (2010). Female Empowerment: Impact of a Commitment Savings Product in the Philippines. *World Development Vol. 38, No. 3*, pp. 333–344.

Bajracharya, A., & Amin, S. (2010). *Poverty, Micro-credit Program Membership and Domestic Violence in Bangladesh: A Study using Propensity Score Matching*. Paper presented at the Seminar on the Population Council's Global Program on Poverty, Gender and Youth. Dhaka, Bangladesh. March 4th, 2010.

Berger, M. (1989). Giving Women Credit: The Strengths and Limitations of Credit as a Tool for Alleviating Poverty. *World Development, 17:7, July*, pp. 1017-32.

Besley, T., & Coate, S. (1995). Group Lending, Repayment Incentives and Social Collateral. *Journal of Development Economics, 46,* pp. 1-18.

Bruce, M. L., Takeuchi, D. T., & Leaf, P. J. (1991). Poverty and Psychiatric Status. *Archives of General Psychiatry, 48,* pp. 470–74.

Cartwright, J., Khandker, S. R., & Pitt, M. M. (2003). Does micro-credit empower women? Evidence from Bangladesh. *World Bank Policy Research* , Working Paper 2998, March.

Chen, J., Choi, Y. J., & Sawada, Y. (2010). Joint liability borrowing and suicide: the case of Japan. *Economics letters, 109,* pp. 69-71.

Diop-Sidibe, N. (2001). *Domestic Violence against Women in Egypt- Risk factors and Health Outcomes of Wife Beating*. Baltimore: The John Hopkins University School of Public Health.

Dohn, A. L., Chávez, A., Dohn, M. N., Saturria, L., & Pimentel, C. (2004). Changes in health indicators related to health promotion and microcredit programs in the Dominican Republic. *Pan American Journal of Public Health, Mar;15(3),* pp. 185-93.

Doocy, S., Teferra, S., Norell, D., & Burnham, G. (2005). Credit program outcomes: coping capacity and nutritional status in the food insecure context of Ethiopia. *Social Science & Medicine. May; 60(10),* pp. 2371-82.

Ellsberg, M., Heise, L., Pena, R., Agurto, S., & Winkvist, A. (2001). Researching domestic violence against women: methodological and ethical considerations. *Studies in Family Planning, Vol.32, No.1*, pp. 1-16.

Exner, T., Hoffman, S., Dworkin, S., & Ehrhardt, A. A. (2003). Beyond the male condom: The evolution of gender-specific HIV interventions for women. *Annual Review of Sex Research, 14,* pp. 114–136.

Frankenberg, E. & Thomas, D. (2001). Women's health and pregnancy outcomes: Do services make a difference? *Demography, 38(2)*, pp. 253–265.

Garikipati, S. (2008). The Impact of Lending to Women on Household Vulnerability and Women's Empowerment: Evidence from India. *World Development, Vol. 36, No. 12,* pp. 2620-264.

Gater, R., Tansella, M., Korten, A., Tiemens, B. G., Mavreas, V. G., & Olatawura, M. O. (1998). Sex differences in the prevalence and detection of depressive and anxiety disorders in general health care settings. *Archives of General Psychiatry, 55,* pp. 405-413.

Ghatak, M., & Guinnane, T. (1999). The Economics of Lending with Joint Liability: Theory and Practice. *Journal of Development Economics, 60 (1),* pp. 95-229.

Ginè, X., & Karlan, D. (2007). *Group versus Individual Liability: A Field Experiment in the Philippines.* Mimeo: Yale University & Innovations for Poverty Action.

Goetz, A. M., & SenGupta, R. (1996). Who Takes the Credit? Gender, power and control over loan use in rural credit programs in Bangladesh. *World Development, 24(1),* pp. 45-64.

Gommans, C. (2006). *Partners and action: Financial institutions and health, HIV & AIDS risk management.* Paper presented at risk management of HIV/AIDS conference, Cape Town, South Africa, April 24, 2006.

Grieg, F. E., & Koopman, C. (2003). Multilevel analysis of women's empowerment and HIV prevention: Quantitative survey results from a preliminary study in Botswana. *AIDS and Behavior, 7,* pp. 195–208.

Hadi, A. (2000). Prevalence and Correlates of the Risk of Marital Sexual Violence in Bangladesh. *Journal of Interpersonal Violence, August vol. 15, no. 8,* pp. 787-805.

Hadi, A. (2001). Promoting health knowledge through micro-credit programmes: Experience of BRAC in Bangladesh. *Health Promotion International, Volume: 16,* pp. 219-227.

Hadi, A. (2005). Women's Productive Work and Marital Violence in Bangladesh. *Journal of Family Violence, 20, No 3,* pp. 181-189.

Hallman, K. (2004). Socioeconomic disadvantage and unsafe sexual behaviors among young women and men in South Africa. *Policy research division working paper no. 190.* New York: Population Council.

Hargreaves, J. R., Pronyk, P. M., & Kim, J.C. (2006). Effect of a structural intervention for the prevention of intimate partner violence and HIV in rural South Africa: results of a duster randomized trial. *Lancet, 368,* pp. 1973-1983.

Hashemi, S. M., & Schuler S. R. (1996). *Sustainable Banking with the Poor: A Case Study of Grameen Bank.* Dhaka: Draft Manuscript.

Hashemi, S. M., Schuler, S. R., & Riley, A. P. (1996). Rural Credit Programs and Women's Empowerment in Bangladesh. *World Development, 24(4)*, pp. 635-654.

Hashemi, S. M, (1997). *Building Capacity for Banking with the Poor: The Grameen Bank in Bangladesh*. In S. Hartmut (Ed.), *Microfinance for the Poor?* (pp.109-126). Paris: Development Centre OECD and IFAD.

Heise, L. (1997). Violence Against Women: An Integrated, Ecological Model. *World Bank Working Paper*. Washington, DC: The World Bank.

Khatun, M., Wadud, N., Bhuiya, A., & Chowdhury, M. (1998). Psychological well-being of rural women: developing measuring tools. *Working Paper No. 23*. Dhaka: BRAC–ICDDR, B Joint Research Project.

Koenig, M. A., Ahmed, S., Hossain, M. B., & Khorshed Alam Mozumder, A. B. M. (2003). Women's status and domestic violence in rural Bangladesh: individual-and community-level effects. *Demography*, *40*, p. 269.

Mayoux, L., (1998).Women's empowerment and micro-finance programmes: strategies for increasing impact. *Development in Practice, 8(2)*, pp. 235-241.

Mohindra, K. S., Haddad, S., & Narayana, D. (2008). Can microcredit help improve the health of poor women? Some finding from a cross-sectional study in Kerala, India. *International Journal for Equity in Health, 7*: 2.

Nanda, P. (1999). *Women's participation in rural credit programmes in Bangladesh and their demand for formal health care: Is there a positive impact?* Center for Health and Gender Equity, Takoma Park.

Olson, M. (1965). *The Logic of Collective Action: Public Goods and the Theory of Groups*. Harvard: Harvard University Press.

OMS, (2001) *Rapport sur la santé dans le monde 2001:La santé mentale, nouvelle conception, nouveaux espoirs*. Organisation Mondiale de la Santé.

Patel, V., & Kleinman, A. (2003). Poverty and common mental disorders in developing countries. *Bulletin of the World Health Organization, 81*, pp. 609-615.

Patel, et al. (2010). Poverty and common mental disorders in low and middle income countries: A systematic review. *Social Science & Medicine 71*, pp. 517-528.

Pitt, M. M., & Khandker, S. R. (1995). *Household and Intrahousehold Impacts of the Grameen Bank and Similar Targeted Credited Programs in Bangladesh*. World Bank, Education and Social Policy Department, Washington. D.C.

Pitt, M. M., & Khandker, S. R. (1998). The impact of group-based credit programs on poor households in Bangladesh: Does the gender of participants matter?. *The Journal of Political Economy, 106 5*, pp. 958–996.

Pitt, M. (1999). *Reply to Jonathan Morduch's. Does Microfinance Really Help the Poor? New Evidence from Flagship Programs in Bangladesh.* Department of Economics. Brown University.

Rahman, A., (1999). Micro-Credit Initiatives For Equitable And Sustainable Development: Who Pays? *World Development, 27*, pp. 67-82.

Rahman, R. I. (1986). Impact of Grameen Bank on the Situation of Poor Rural Women. *Working Paper No.1*, Grameen Bank Evaluation Project. BIDS, Dhaka.

Schuler, S. R., Hashemi, S. M., Badal, S. H. (1998). Men's violence against women in rural Bangladesh: undermined or exacerbated by microcredit programs? *Development in Practice, 8,* pp. 148-157.

Schuler S. R., Hashemi, S. M., Riley A. P., & Akhter, S. (1996). Credit programs, patriarchy, and men's violence against women in rural Bangladesh. *Social Science & Medicine; 43,* pp. 1729-1742.

Tajfel, H. (1981). *Human Groups and Social Categories. Studies in Social Psychology.* Cambridge: Cambridge University Press.

Woolcock, M. J. V. (1999). Learning from failures in microfinance: What unsuccessful cases tell us about how group-based programs work? *American Journal of Economics and Sociology, Vol 58, Issue 1,* pp. 17–42.

In: The Other Side of the Coin
Editors: L. Brunori and M. Pines
ISBN: 978-1-62618-726-9

Chapter 6

FAMILY NETWORK AND HOUSEHOLD DECISION MAKING POWER: ANALYSIS ON GRAMEEN MICROCREDIT BORROWERS IN BANGLADESH

Giorgia Bonaga and Md Shamimur Rahman
Department of Psychology, University of Bologna, Italy

ABSTRACT

Microcredit, a system of small loans, invests in the creativity of an individual, stimulating the development of their potential. This process leads to the creation of different objectives that, in turn, allow individuals to develop their capabilities.

In addition to providing economic benefits, microfinance may be an effective vehicle for women's empowerment, and newly acquired business skills may be accompanied by improvements in self-esteem, the ability to resolve conflicts, household decision making power, and improve the quality of family relationships.

The aim of this study was to evaluate the effectiveness of microcredit intervention, in terms of improving the economic well-being of women and their families, and increasing benefits in terms of individual welfare, family and society. It is therefore an impact assessment study that aims to detect a significant change on new women borrowers' lives from Noakhali District at the South of Bangladesh.

Manova Analysis allowed distinguishing from women with positive or negative outcomes related to the loan performance. Data revealed consistent differences in terms of economical outcomes and psychological well-being amongst the groups of subject analyzed. In this chapter we will present the preliminary results regarding the family well-being detected by two indicators: the household decision-making power and the quality of family relationships. The data gathered in relation to the changes arisen in the individuals should be looked into through future, continuous and systematic, monitoring.

INTRODUCTION

Microcredit is a tool of economic development that aids people living in poverty to access those financial services that, normally, would be denied.

At the end of 2005, nominated as the International Year of Microcredit, the Microcredit Summit Campaign, a UN project, publicizes its latest report:" According to data collected from about 3,000 microfinance institutions, 92 million people were reached by microcredit projects around the world, at the end of 2004, it is estimated that 66, 6 million of which were the poorest families, those living on less than a dollar a day." However, the goal of the Campaign on Microcredit is even more ambitious: to reach 175 million of the poorest families in the world by the end of 2015.

It is therefore understandable that the enthusiasm may have encouraged huge expectations about the Microcredit tool.

In recent years many researchers presented to the scientific community impact assessments studies with seemingly contradictory findings.

It stands to reason that for understanding and evaluating the complexity of such phenomenon and its multiple variables involved, it is necessary to draw from different theoretical constructs, methodologies and research tools from various fields of study (psychology, economics, anthropology, sociology, etc.)

This is the reason why we conducted the present study within a group of multi-disciplinary research.

This has allowed us to observe the impact of microcredit and therefore the change of individuals from three different disciplines' points of view: Psychology, Economics and Sociology.

The results obtained are discussed in relation to the main data in the literature that have focused on the effect of micro-credit program in Developing Countries.

Far from offering the last word on the impact of microfinance, the present study provides a basis to rather watch the process of change of the individual from a purely psychological point of view and to understand how the device works, for whom and circumstances under which the loans are able to offer the greatest potential beneficiaries of development.

BACKGROUND

Microcredit and Household Decision Making Power

Some authors believe that microcredit has helped women to increase revenue opportunities, their level of self-confidence and confidence in others, and the ability to overcome cultural asymmetries (Rahman, 1986; Hashemi, Schuler, & Riley, 1996; Pitt & Khandker, 1998; Kabeer, 2001; Pitt, Khandker & Cartwright, 2006). However, other authors believe that loans granted to women are actually managed by their husbands, a situation that could lead to an increase in dependence on them as far as loan installments are concerned, and an exacerbation of pre-existing internal conflicts and incidents of domestic violence (Goetz & SenGupta, 1996; Rahman, 1999; Leach & Sitaram, 2002).

There are several studies that examine the influence of microcredit on female empowerment (Kabeer, 2001) and most of them, thanks to mainly observational and qualitative methods, outline a very positive impact of microcredit on women's lives. Rahman R.I. (1986) found that women taking part in microcredit programs, beside having an income and a consumption rate higher when compared to that of families that do not participate, play an important role in decision-making within the household.

Pitt and Khandker (1995) have measured the impact of microcredit programs on gender identity based on a series of indicators of empowerment. The results showed that, within families involved in microcredit programs, there is more gender equity compared to the other families in which, on the contrary, the women's opinion is taken into little consideration.

Microcredit and Household Relationships

Although several studies have clearly found some positive effects of participation in microcredit groups on domestic violence, the scientific debate recently has been promoted by further studies that have raised serious concerns following the detection of an increased incidence of gender-based violence among women in microcredit programs (Koenig, Ahmed, Hossain & Mazumdar, 2003).

In light of unquestionable results, Schuler et al. (1996) suggest that membership in a microcredit organization is associated with a reduced risk of suffering domestic violence. The study showed a reduction in the levels of violence in two thirds of the families involved in microcredit programs, compared to the families which were not involved. In addition, these positive effects seem to include women who are not members, but who live in villages where microcredit programs are employed.

On the other hand, extensive qualitative studies present more ambiguous results. A study by Schuler et al. (1998) showed that microcredit could exacerbate domestic violence. The violence within families may get worse if the fact of belonging to the group encourages women to challenge traditional gender roles and to maintain control over the resources that are traditionally managed by their husbands. As soon as the husband realizes that the authoritarian control over his wife is compromised because she is a member of a group, the violence increases.

The acquisition of a greater autonomy in economic and social terms would encourage women to gain power within the decision-making by challenging male authority and providing reasons to exacerbate marital and familiar conflict.

However, other studies, including those of Jewkes (2002) and Koenig et al. (2003), have shown the possibility in which the increments of recorded violence can constitute short-term reactions caused by the initial shock that participation to such programs involves, compared to traditional gender norms. These negative effects, however, may decrease in the long term as a result of the increase in the level of women empowerment. In a long-term, the group membership tends to be a protective factor from gender-based violence (World Bank, 2009).

On the basis of these contradictory evidences, the development of a conclusive hypothesis about the possibility that microcredit could influence domestic violence remains therefore mainly unsolved.

Gender Management of the Loan

Some studies have also found a negative impact on the empowerment of women. Most of these studies focused on the level of women's control of loans. Goetz and Sengupta (1996), analyzing the index management control of loans, found that the majority of married women have a very limited control, sometimes non-existent control, upon loans (Montgomery, Bhattacharya & Hulme, 1996).

This has a negative influence on the repayment process, because when the repayment responsibility is controlled by men and they show a poor capability to face up to it, conflicts light up in the household, thus frustrating all development objectives underlying the practice of microcredit.

Other authors believe that loans to women are in general totally controlled by their husbands. This situation could lead to an increase in the degree of dependence on them and to episodes of internal conflict and violence during the repayment process (Rahman, 1999; Leach & Sitaram, 2002).

AIMS AND HYPOTHESIS OF CURRENT STUDY

Microcredit, a small lending system, invests on an individual's creativity by stimulating the development of their own potential. This process leads to the attainment of various objectives which in turn allows individuals to develop their skill awareness. Consequently, this process also increases individual empowerment and sense of agency. These factors play an important role in the etiology of a number of mental disorders such as depression and anxiety. Namely, those characterized by a series of psychological conditions which impede the full development of a person's personal, relational and social sphere.

From this perspective, Microcredit is seen as a form of intervention to be integrated within traditional forms to promote developing countries' Family Planning and Mental Health Programs. As such, financial independency is promoted in people who are normally excluded from the working circuit by giving them the opportunity of measuring themselves as active agents primarily within their family and secondly within their Community.

Furthermore, since Microcredit is thought to produce tangible goods, such as income, and intangible goods, such as self-esteem and mutual trust, it could also represent an innovative socio-economic tool.

In addition to providing economic benefits, microfinance may be an effective vehicle for women's empowerment, and newly acquired business skills may be accompanied by improvements in psychological well-being, the ability to resolve conflicts, household decision making power, and improved the quality of family relationships.

These considerations are reflected in the study below, where microcredit is considered on one hand as an inexpensive tool that can help families emerge from poverty and on the other as an interesting solution for people exposed to stress caused by adverse economic conditions by helping them avoid the risk of domestic violence and mental disorders.

The aim of this study is to evaluate the effectiveness of Microcredit intervention by considering the increased economic and family well-being observed in the subjects involved within their individual, family and realms.

As such, the change we are expecting to perceive in the subjects of this study is understood as a development of their "capabilities" (Sen, 1982). The expected results will fall under and refer to two main aspects:

1. Intangible Aspect: in terms of improved quality of family relationships and increased wife decision making power;
2. Tangible Aspect: in terms of improving their quality of household life and having successfully conducted their family business.

METHOD

Participants

Participants included women participating in Grameen Bank programmes (N 100). Borrowers were recruited from three different villages in the District of Noakhali in Bangladesh: branch 1, Mokra Nangolot (29.4%), branch 2, Dhaulo (22.4%), branch 3, Feria (48.2%).

As this study was carried out over a specific one year period from February 2010 (*baseline:* time 0) to February 2011 (*outcome:* time 1), the participants included where the ones who, during the full period, adhered to the microcredit group program.

15 subjects dropped-out between time 0 (baseline) and time 1 (outcome). These people were untraceable or no longer available at the time of the second inquiry.

The convenience sampling was composed exclusively of women joining the Grameen microcredit program. The subjects were selected solely on the basis of their status as new beneficiaries (defined new borrowers) participating in the program for credit up to 3 months. At the time of selection, women who benefited from other development programs (micro-individual, government programs, etc.) were also excluded.

The average age of the study sample was 33,18 years (± 9,17; range: 19-57).

To meet the above inclusion criteria, the local operators of the Grameen Bank selected the more remote villages where the likelihood of detecting neo-beneficiaries was higher.

In the research design a control group was not included for a number of reasons:

1. Objective difficulties in finding women excluded from development programs. Within the same village, in fact, there are many microfinance institutions with different methodologies and financial services ;
2. Ethical issue related to the impossibility of the control group to adhere to any development or credit program during the 12 month period of the research;
3. The essentially exploratory nature of the study which presents itself as a pilot project aimed at testing *Household Decision Making Power tool* (DMP) in an evaluation study of the economic impact.

However, in order to obtain the parameters of economic welfare of comparison, the assessment evaluation tool was also administered to 32 women whom have been taking part in the microcredit program of the Grameen Bank (defined old borrowers) for over 10 years. The analysis carried out between the two study groups are not reflected in this chapter, but have been used to understand the range of economic and psychological well-being present within the same community-village of the reference sample.

Profile of Sample

The interviews were conducted in the district of Noakhali, a region in the South of Bangladesh, namely 27 different villages where covered by 3 branch offices of the Grameen Bank.

This is a particularly precarious area, the survival of which is entrusted mainly to an agricultural subsistence economy. The villages of the region are remote, sparsely equipped with infrastructure and with limited opportunities for communication power supply. More than half of the population has no formal education, and over 80% are Muslim. The isolation of these villages has led to a particularly conservative and male-dominated culture. These villages can be considered broadly representative of rural Bangladesh.

Usually in Bangladesh in the villages women get married at the age of 14 to 16 in most cases. There are several reasons to it. For a typical agrarian society women were seen as a productive force of making children. Son is expected as they will work in the field. Women are treated like a liability as it takes a lot of money or other goods to get them married as a dowry. As the women marry early, they usually spend the adolescent age in her husband's house. And the friendship among school friends or friends from the neighbors never really blossoms because of the short period they spend with them. Once they get married and come to a new house, they develop a relationship among the household members. The household members consist of several individual, mostly in laws. They are used to have few activities outside the household. So, they do not usually have a great social life outside of it. They usually attend the marriage and other ceremonies close to their house or if the persons who are getting married are very close to them. Most of the activities of them surround in taking care of the children, cooking and cleaning. They also bring food for their husband if the husband works in the field.

Often men are needed to manage the purchasing and selling process and women raise milk cow and take care of animal husbandry. Women neither run shops nor do they go for buying from the market. In the celebration period, sometimes they accompany their men to buy clothes for their children.

Experimental Design

The study falls in the drawings almost experimental because it is characterized by the partial control of all the variables in play. It is characterized by a single sample, on which were carried out repeated measurements according to a longitudinal research design.

The entire system was subjected to the evaluation phase of back translation and pre-made test (January 2010) on a dummy sample of 32 women who received a microcredit program. After the adaptation stage of the tools to the specific cultural context (focus groups were held with key people in the community: local leaders, teachers and religious leaders), we proceeded with the first inquiry (February 2010) on new borrowers. The second inquiry was made on the same subject-group with the same tools after 12 months (February 2011)

All interviews were conducted in private at the homes of the beneficiaries. The information was collected through individual interview, which lasted an average of about 45 minutes. Every effort was made to ensure privacy during the interviews and to suspend discussion of sensitive topics when interruptions could not be avoided. Respondents of each family were guaranteed confidentiality of the process and outcomes. If the selected person was not at home, additional visits were made.

Outcome Measures

In order to understand and assess the impact of microcredit program participation has been necessary to consider all the many variables involved in the process of change.

We interpreted the microcredit program as a sort of therapeutic path, as a transitional space through which the borrower could become an empowered woman. This is the reason why draw on therapeutic tools generally used for the evaluation of the group psychotherapies outcomes, focusing the interest on the analysis of family and relational realms of individuals (intangible dimension).

Furthermore, in order to assess the effects of micro-credit program on economic well-being (tangible dimension), we referred to literature and the traditional methods used to measure the microfinance impact. In this study it was necessary to harmonize the dialogue between very different disciplines such as psychology and economics, preferring multidisciplinary assessment tools capable of returning a complete picture of all aspects involved.

All instruments have been adapted to the specific context, both through the traditional method of back translation, and through discussions and focus groups with beneficiaries of micro-credit programs and members of the local community.

Household Decision Making Process Questionnaire

To assess the distribution of decision-making power within the family we made a questionnaire with 25 items: the Household Decisional Making Process Questionnaire (HDPQ).

The questionnaire responses provide information on the percentage of decisions taken independently by the wife, by the husband, by husband and wife jointly and by other family members (i.e. son, mother in law, father in law). The 25 items investigate five aspects: the generational issues (G), economical issues (E), fulfillment of basic needs issues (B), community issues (C) and recreational issues (R). All five dimensions are divided into Internal Issues (i) (i.e. decisions relating to the problems within the family) and External Issues (e) (i.e. decisions relating to the problems outside the family) allowing to discriminate between internal decision-making and external decision-making. All items were discussed with local representatives and with a group of 32 beneficiaries of the Grameen program during the pre-test and appropriately adapted to the context.

Family Network

The aim of this work is to analyze the family relationships of the beneficiaries of microcredit Grameen Programme. The instrument chosen in this study is the "network chart", a technique of mind-imaging derived from modern sociological research on social networks (Social Network), which represents graphically, with specific symbols, relational networks of the subject and the subjective reconstruction of his way of living in the world.

Table 2. Household Decision Making Power Questionnaire

Who decides about what.....			**Wife**	**Husband**	**Others**
Gi	1	Who takes the decision of who will take care of the old people at home?			
Gi	2	Who takes the decision to teach children at home?			
Ge	3	Who takes the decision to go to the hospital, if someone is ill in the family?			
Gi	4	Who takes the decision to give birth to a baby?			
Gi	5	Who gives the name to a newborn baby?			
Ei	6	Who takes the decision of who will take care of the business activity at home?			
Ei	7	Who takes the decision of who will have control over the money or profit from the business?			
Ee	8	Who takes the decision to take a loan from the bank?			
Ee	9	Who takes the decision about what to			

Who decides about what…..			Wife	Husband	Others
		do with the loan and how and where to invest it?			
Ee	10	Who takes the decision to buy new property and who will be the owner of it?			
Ei	11	Who takes decision to buy seeds and plant them?			
Bi	12	Who takes the decision to make a new house or repairing it or make new rooms?			
Bi	13	Who takes the decision to buy new clothes for the families?			
Be	14	Who takes the decision involving schooling of the children?			
Be	15	Who takes the decision to go to the school to pay for the fees?			
Ci	16	Who takes the decision to buy gifts for different ceremonies?			
Ce	17	Who takes the decision to solve internal problems of the neighbours?			
Ce	18	Who takes the decision to go and protect neighbours from moneylenders or dowries or other external problems?			
Ce	19	Who takes the decision to participate in the election?			
Ce	20	Who takes the decision to vote for particular political parties?			
Ri	21	Who takes the decision to buy a Television or radio or other objects for home?			
Re	22	Who takes the decision to go for a vacation?			
Ri	23	Who takes the decision to invite other people at home?			
Re	24	Who takes the decision to go watching a movie or circus or plays or festivals?			
Re	25	Who takes the decision to send children for parties and other activities?			

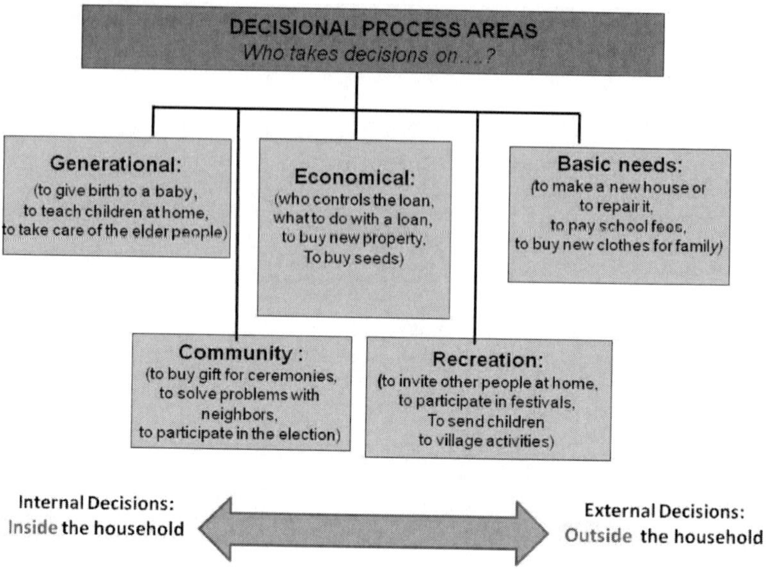

Figure 8. Structure of Household Decision Making Power Questionnaire.

Through the construction of a kind of relational map, it becomes possible to graph and visualize social networks and interpersonal ties of the subject. The ego-centered position of the subject displays the disposition of its networks and the weaving of direct links between him and the others.

It is considered, in the context of group psychotherapy, a useful tool to evaluate and monitoring patient's relational aspects of their mental functioning.

In order to represent the change of household relational map we used the method of Multidimensional Scaling (MDS) and in particular the model in Euclidean distance (ALSCAL) that allows efficient representation also in the case of a few variables.

The Multidimensional Scaling (MDS Multidimensional Scaling) is a technique of statistical analysis of the data that allows obtaining a representation of n objects in a space with k dimensions, starting from information relating to the "similarity" (or dissimilarity) between each pair of the n objects. Generally, it is a technique used to display the (dis)similarity (distance) between objects in a small space (often 2D or 3D).

CGAP Poverty Assessment Tool and Grameen Form 1

To assess the economic well-being it has been used CGAP Poverty Assessment Tool (PAT) designed to offer a clear picture on the poverty level of their clients. It provides rigorous data on poverty levels of clients, as members of a specific community, thanks to the ad hoc construction of a multidimensional poverty index that allows comparisons between MFI outcomes in different countries.

The family is the basic unit of sampling. Generally applies only to new beneficiaries (less than six months into the program), in order to eliminate any variables covariates related to adherence to long development program.

The tool collects information about the different dimensions of poverty. The indicators are:

- demographic structure and economic activities
- footwear and clothing expenses
- food security and vulnerability: the frequency of meals, consumption of luxury and inferior food, days without food
- status of home ownership, room size, building material, access to electricity, clean water and sanitation, cooking fuel
- land ownership
- total value of property: assets, livestock, production and consumer goods

To implement the collection of economical household data at baseline time, we used Information provided by the Grameen Form 1, the main questionnaire used by Grameen loan officers to collect preliminary data for new Clients.

Details of the subjects' demographic and socio-economic characteristics were ascertained through questions about age, educational attainment, marital status, number of children, husband's main occupation, monthly household income, household quality and size.

Business Performance

We included other items focused on business performance in order to detect some discriminating variables about success or failure of the microcredit program participation:

In particular, the indicators were:

1. user loan
2. level of women's control of loans
3. size of loan

4. type of loan (properly loan)
5. type of business (loan investment patterns)
6. performance repayment of the loan
7. outcome of business
8. overlapping

A range of questions were asked about women's use loan (1) and level of women's control loan (2). These indicators have been added to investigate the issues of "gender management of loan".

Few evaluations of loan use investigate whether women actually control this credit. The literature highlights (Rahman R., 1986; White, 1991; Ackerly, 1995; Goetz & SenGupta, 1996) the issue of transfer of loan control from women borrowers to their husband or other male relatives (i.e. sons, nephews, sons in law).

Furthermore, findings show that even though women are using loan by themselves, they have a limited control over the management of productive process and the use of profits.

The indicators relating to the size of loan (3), type of loan (4) and Type of business (loan investment patterns) (5) have been added to identify the loans improperly invested, that are not directed to any business, but rather to practical extinction of earlier loans, to payments for dowry or for a migrant member of the family. The following indicators Performance repayment of the loan (6) and Outcome of business (degree of increase in household incomes) (7) allow the monitoring of the whole process and to discriminate against beneficiaries who have failed to repay or to invest the loan. Outcome of business indicates the success of the investment, not just in the degree of increase in household incomes, but rather in the sense of completeness of the business project and complete return of the loan.

Finally, the last point (8) alerted us to the phenomenon of loan overlapping that could be responsible for the development goals failure of microcredit programs.

Statistical Methods

All statistical analysis were performed with the statistical software package SPSS, version 19 for Windows operating system.

After checking that the assumptions of their statistical tests were met:

- Multivariate Analysis were performed for repeated tests to detect the change between the first (Time 0) and the second inquiry (Time 1), T test for paired samples for continuous variables, Wilcoxon test for ordinal variables and McNemar test for dichotomous variables.
- factor Analysis Mixed Analysis and RM Manova were performed to detect the effect of the performance outcome of microcredit, the time effect and the interaction effect between these two factors;
- the analysis of the quality of relationship family and social of the beneficiaries were conducted through the technique of Multidimensional Scaling (MDS ALSCAL Model Euclidean Distances)
- linear regressions were performed to detect the intertwining between the size of the tangible and intangible dimension
- Pearson's Chi Square test and Mann Whitney test were performed for independent samples t test to detect individual differences and family between the two different outcome groups (positive and negative outcomes).

The design is factorial, as are all the possible combinations of factors and it was possible to analyze all the effects as well as all the classification criteria used and all the possible interactions between the main effects.

The process of interpretation of the results developed in parallel with a constant and continuous study of the results emerging in the scientific literature devoted to analysis of the impact of microcredit programs.

RESULTS

Business Performance

User Loan and Level of Women's Control of Loans

All analysis of the business performance change (improvement or deterioration) were made only on the members who remained active throughout the research period (N 72).

From the descriptive analysis we note that after 12 months increases both the percentage of women using the loan by itself (Time 0: 15.3%; Time 1: 26.4%) and the percentage of households in which both spouses used jointly the loan (Time 0: 11.1%; Time 1: 19.4%). No difference in the relative proportions of those who actually manages the loan, loan management is distributed among total control of her husband and joint management of husband and wife.

		Time 0		Time 1	
Loan User		**N**	**%**	**N**	**%**
	Husband	48	66,7%	36	50,0%
	Wife	11	15,3%	19	26,4%
	Son	5	6,9%	3	4,2%
	Husband & Wife	8	11,1%	14	19,4%
	Total	72	100%	72	100%
		Time 0		**Time 1**	
Loan Control		N	%	N	%
	Husband	25	34,7%	25	34,7%
	Wife	21	29,2%	20	27,8%
	Son	2	2,8%	1	1,4%
	Husband & Wife	24	33,3%	26	36,1%
	Total	72	100%	72	100%

With regard to the actual loan user and the level of women's loan control, a few considerations should be made. It is important to note that the strict rules of the social and cultural context examined considerably hamper the independent and direct management of the business by women. In rural areas, it is difficult to see women manage their business on their own, whether it being a shop, the livestock market or a restaurant kitchen. Often they cannot show themselves in public without being accompanied by their husbands; they do not handle money and are not able to count the income and expenditure of the family business. For these reasons, there is often a shift of the loan directly from the hands of the wife to the hands of the husband. Our data, in agreement with the literature, has found a high percentage of husbands who use the loan directly, without any involvement of the wives in the business. In addition, if the loan is used by both spouses or only by women, the scope for action of the beneficiary remains severely restricted. Women's economic activities are limited to the perimeter of the village to which they belong and must require the contribution of a husband or son. Generally the woman is responsible for activities such as care for and feeding of pets, tailoring and packaging of dresses and seasonal cultivation of family land. The products, the result of the work of wives, will then be put on the market by the husband who will negotiate the price and conclude the deal.

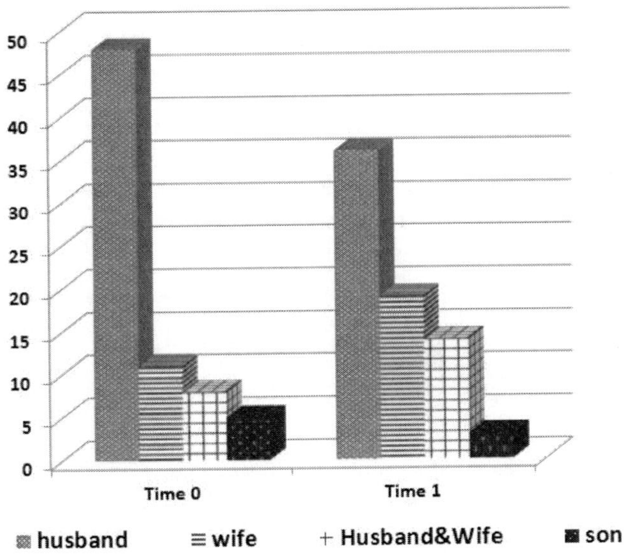

Figure 9. User loan.

As already pointed out, the literature reports different opinions about the actual and exclusive management of the loan by wives in developing countries. Even where the wife was the sole user and beneficiary of the loan it would not be so obvious to expect that it was the sole administrator. For the reasons described above, the need for the woman to ask her husband to mediate between its business and the external market often requires having to settle for a subordinate position in the family decision-making process regarding the investment of the loan. Since she is not in the best condition to use and manage the loan independently, they often delegate the management to their husband or male child, thus affecting the assumption of gender empowerment underlying the micro device.

The results of this study confirm this hypothesis, indicating that the percentage of use and management of the loan are distributed mostly in favor of the husband. However, at a distance of 12 months from access to credit program, there was an increase in both the percentage of women using the loan themselves and in the percentage of households in which the loan is used jointly by both spouses. The same change occurs in the percentages of actual management of the loan, which despite being majorly in favor of men, in the second inquiry; it increases in favor of a joint management of the loan.

Loan Size

At the end of the first cycle of repayment of the loan, most of the beneficiaries requested a second loan for an amount greater than the previous (Time 0: M = 8.555,56 Tk; Time 1: M = 12.763,89 Tk), this variation is generally indicator of the success of the credit program. A small percentage (9.4%) of the subjects left the program after having completed the first cycle of loans with Grameen. The abandonment of the program may depend on a wide variety of reasons: the need of the family to move to another village, the change in the family structure as a result of divorce or voluntary departure of a spouse.

Outcome of Business

To evaluate the performance of the loan a very important variable was taken into consideration: the outcome of the loan (i.e. the outcome of the investment credit).

The outcome was calculated on the basis of the wealth acquired by individual families during the 12-month program. The outcome was defined as successful (Success) by virtue of the increased value of their holdings (61%, M), and was defined as negative (failure) as a result of the decrease or no enhancement of the value of their possessions (39%). The application of this differentiation has allowed us to measure the consequences of different business performance.

The discussion of the results presented below will therefore analyze the impact of microcredit by always taking into account both the samples as a whole. Namely, by distinguishing between borrowers with positive outcomes (those who became wealthier as a result of a good loan investment) and borrowers with negative outcomes (those who did not become wealthier as a result of the investment of the loan).

Tangible Dimension

Value of Property

In relation to acquired wealth a significant effect is detected of the interaction *outcomeXtime* [F (1, 83) = 39.876, p ≤, 0001, η2 partial = ,325], this means that the sole participation in the microcredit program does not significantly change the total value of assets owned, instead it's the success or failure of such participation that determines a significant difference in wealth acquired.

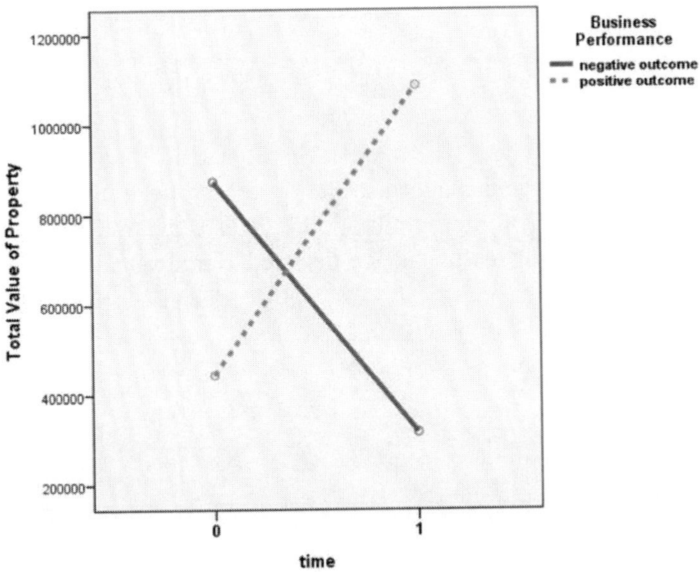

Figure 10. Total value of property.

Relatively to the value of single pattern of property (land, assets, livestock) there are some distinctions: there is a main effect of *time* only on the Assets variable [F (1,83) = 11,173, p ≤ ,001, η2 partial = ,119] and an interaction effect *outcomeXtime* only on the Land variable [F (1,83) = 38,473, p ≤ ,0001, η2 partial = ,317]. This means that all families, regardless of the outcome, have invested in the purchase of household goods (assets) and that during their participation in the microcredit program, families that have been successful have primarily invested in the purchase of property landholdings.

Through the analysis of variance (ANOVA) it was possible to compare the two groups (families with positive outcome and families with negative outcome) at the time of access to micro-credit program: The analysis revealed a significant difference between the two groups regarding the economic value of property in total. Women with negative outcomes, on average, had a total value of property two times greater compared to women with positive outcomes. Families who have failed in the investment of the loan started out from a more economically advantageous condition compared to women who were successful. This starting point of wealth was usually attributed to the possession of estates. There were no significant differences in relation to the total value of animals and assets.

Intangible Dimension

Decision-making Power in the Family

A multivariate analysis of mixed factorial variance was used to detect some changes in the percentage distribution of the decision-making power among the members of the family (Wife, Husband, Wife and Husband together and others). In particular, we detected significant *time* effect [F (1, 73) = 5.926, p ≤ .0001, η2 partial =,243] in the decreased percentage of the decision-making power of the husband [Figure 11], regardless of the outcome of the program [F (1,73) = 6.427, p = ,013, , η2 partial = ,081].

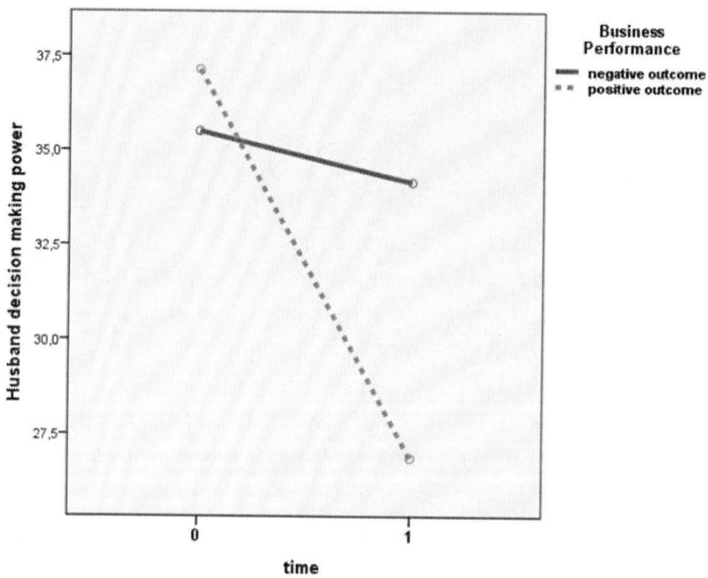

Figure 11. Husband decision making power.

Although it was detected a main effect of *outcome*, the charts show that the distribution of decision-making power in families with failure (negative outcome) remains almost unchanged during the 12 months, while in families with success (positive outcome) major changes were observed and, in particular, an increase in joint decision making and a decrease of husband decision making power. [Figures 11, 12, 13].

At the time of access to credit, families with positive and negative outcomes findings showed no significant differences in the distribution of decision-making power. However, from the descriptive mean it can be deducted that women with negative outcome had a greater decision-making power than women with positive outcomes. The percentage of husbands' decision-making power and shared decision-making power, however, is similar.

By breaking down the overall rates in percentages of decision-making on internal issues *(domestic issues)* and in percentage of decision-making power on external issues *(outside issues)* it was possible to get more detailed information about the real distribution of power in the family. It was clear, in fact, that within the particular cultural context under study, the detection of any increase in the wife decision-making power on issues outside the family (e.g. decision to go to vote, to participate in the activities of the village to interact with institutions), as well as on domestic issues, have more weight and are therefore more important in view of gender empowerment.

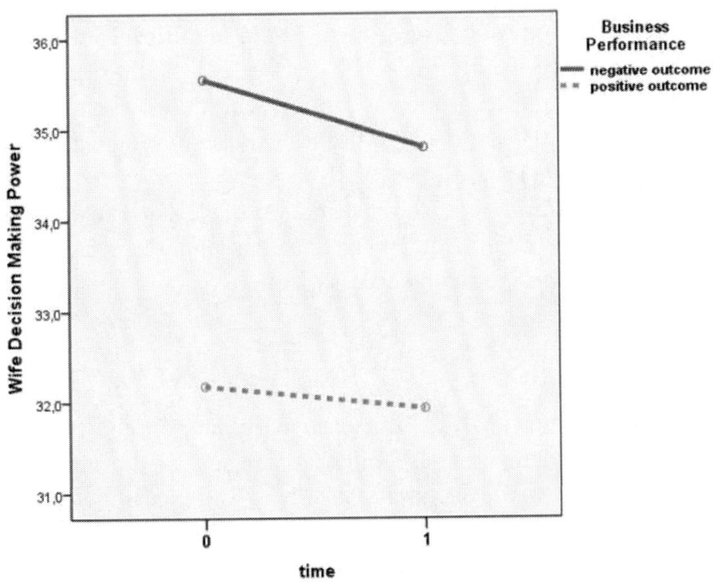

Figure 12. Wife decision making power.

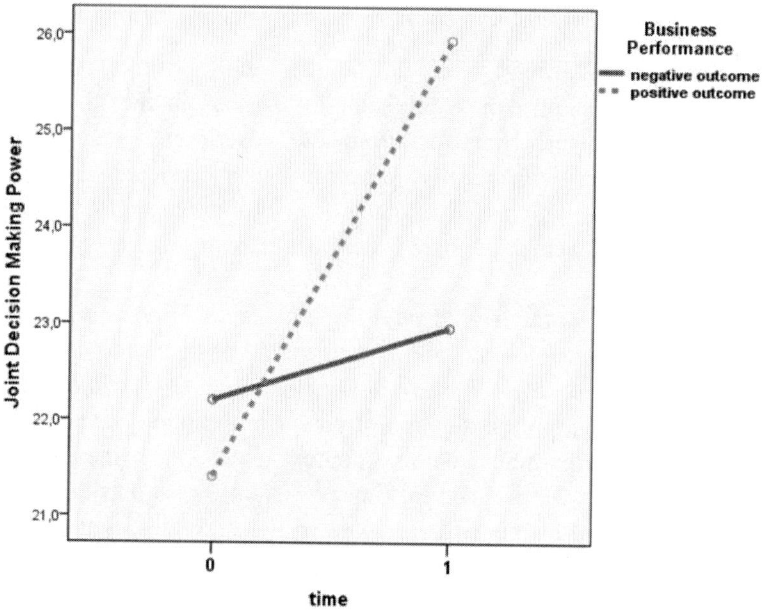

Figure 13. Joint decision making power.

With regard to domestic issues, there was a significant increase in joint decision-making power [t (s) (74) = -2,33, p = ,022]. With regard to external issues, there was a significant increase in the wife decision-making power [t (s) (74) = -2,00, p = ,049] and a significant decrease in the husband decision-making power [t (s) (74) = 2,23, p = ,028].

Similar to domestic issues, the distribution of decision-making power in families with failure (negative outcome) remained almost unchanged over the 12 months, while in families with success (positive outcome) the proportion of joint decisions increased.

Family Relationships

Family relationships analysis was particularly helpful allowing us to map the change within dynamics household. With regard to the number and the relationships quality, mixed factorial analysis of variance showed *time* effect [$F(1, 83) = 26{,}977$, $p \leq {,}0001$, $\eta 2$ partial =,245] as being significantly responsible for the increase in the number of emotionally important family relationships regardless of the business outcome.

The Wilcoxon test also revealed a significant change in the percentage of women who reported deterioration in the quality of the relationship with their husbands (average relationship, weak or interrupted by 7.4% to 24.7%). The biggest changes were detected in the analysis of relational intensity made by the Multidimensional Scaling method. By analyzing the average relational distance of the whole sample, there was an increase in emotional distance for their husbands reported by the women interviewed. If you differ in families with positive and negative outcomes is detected as such emotional distancing, is particularly intense for women with negative outcomes.

A change in the balance of family was detected in a reduction of the decision-making power of the husband and an increase in the proportion of decisions taken in mutual agreement between the spouses.

The following figures refer to maps relatives of women with negative outcomes and positive outcomes.

The first map [Figure 14] shows the emotional distances difference between time 0 *(DI)* and time 1*(DIT1)* in families that have not been successful in following the investment of the loan. We included Husband, Mother, Father, first son and first daughter.

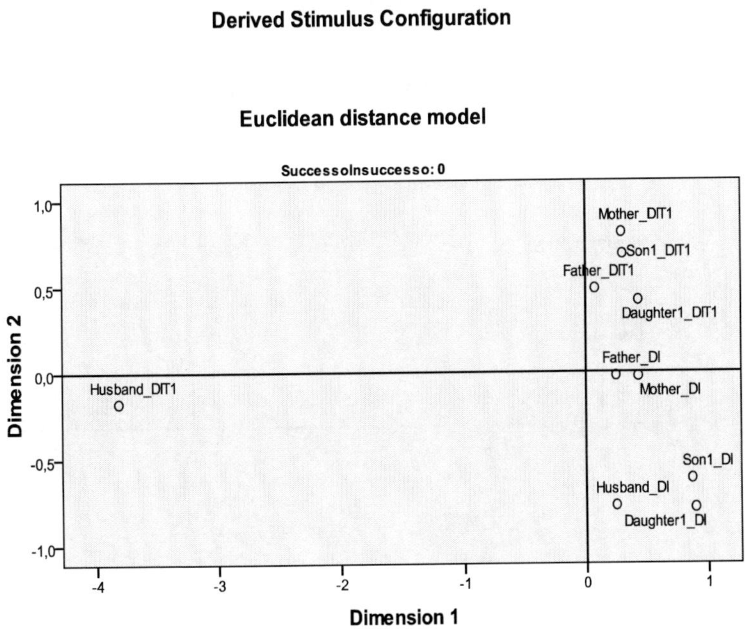

Figure 14. Family network of borrowers with negative outcome.

Notice that, in this particular situation, the affective and relational distance between husband and wife is significantly increased. In fact during the first access to credit the husband stood in the right lower quadrant (*Husband_DI*), close to all the other members, since access to credit, the husband is placed at a great distance from both the wife and the other members (*Husband_DIT1*). Such a removal would seem to indicate the presence of emotional conflict within the family. And 'well-known that, in some cases, the participation of women in development programs leads to an alteration in family dynamics (Jewkes, 2002; Koenig et al., 2003),). In the case of microcredit, in particular, the empowerment of women as beneficiaries of a loan, could significantly disrupt the prior balance of power. The conflict between the spouses may turn on or exacerbate for several reasons: first, because of the limited and sometimes non-existent wife control loan which is solely responsible, and secondly due to obstructive practices implemented by their husbands who wish to take advantage of the economic opportunities by keeping quiet about the duty to repay the loan on time. This is, of course, a negative influence on the process of return and slows the achievement of women's development underlying the practice of credit.

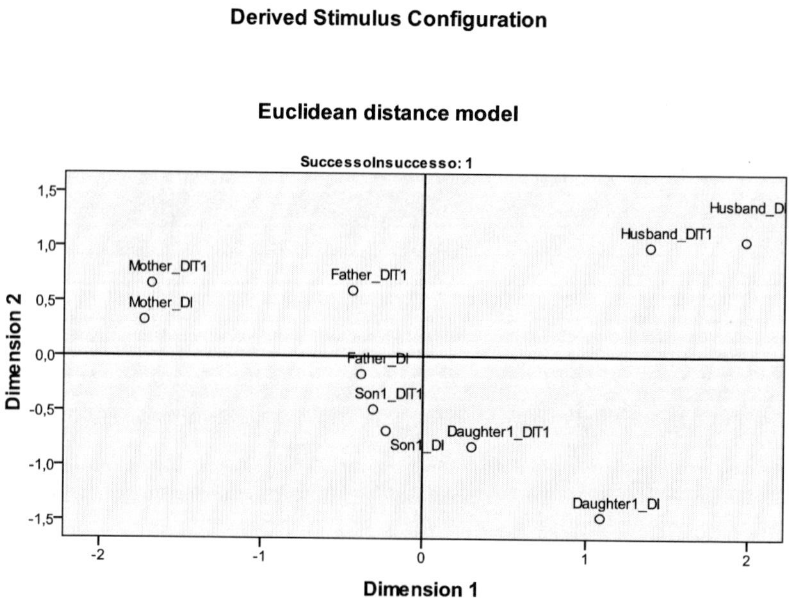

Figure 15. Family Network of borrowers with positive outcome.

The family situation of women who have been successful seems to be very different.

Figure 15 shows a more homogeneous distribution in the four quadrants of the relational distance of family members. In particular, note the location of the husband that, while maintaining a relatively distant position with respect to the wife and the other members of the family, affectively seems closer to the borrower after 12 months from access to credit. This may be primarily a result of improved economic conditions of the family as a result of the member's participation in the microcredit programs. Secondly, the threat of losing the opportunity to receive loans because of the violence may have also led their husbands to become less violent. Finally, the enrichment of the social network of support and acquire the most central place in society earned through participation in groups may have acted as reducers of domestic violence. In any case it is clear that the families who have been successful, they are not characterized by the presence of apparent conflicts.

Note, also, that in these families, unlike those with negative outcome, seems to reduce the relational distance between the borrower and the first daughter. This approximation may be interpreted as the result of 'increased sense of agency of the borrower itself, helping to gradually improve the economic conditions of their families, is perceived as better able to ensure a better future daughters.

DISCUSSION

The results seem to support the hypothesis that adherence to the micro-credit program led to a number of changes in the personal and family life of the beneficiaries. Most of the mixed factorial analysis of variance pointed out that these changes occur often regardless of the outcome of the positive and negative investment loan. By empowering women as beneficiaries of the development program, family and individual dynamics were influenced. In some cases, however, the improvement in quality of life is particularly evident, for example in those families with positive outcomes who invested their loan safely and enjoyed its profits. Until now we could trace a profile of the two types of women: women with negative outcomes appear to be women with a higher decisional making power and more economically prosperous. On the other hand, women with positive outcome, started at a disadvantage both in terms of decisional making power and from an economic point of view. The constellation of psychological and family traits traced so far suggests that women with negative outcome, precisely because of their privileged position of origin in terms of empowerment, have met more resistance from their husband in implementing the path of self-sufficiency. This hypothesis is supported by the evident deterioration in the quality of the relationship with their husbands and by the increase in emotional distance recorded during the 12 months of participation in microcredit program.

In order to exclude the possibility that, between the two types of women, there were the objective characteristics that could have acted as moderator variables or covariates of the outcome, we analyzed the demographic variables and variables related to the performance of the loan.

There were no significant differences between the two types of women with respect to the age and the number of children.

There were no significant differences between women with positive and negative outcomes in relation to husband employment status, marital status and level of education.

Analysis of variance showed no significant difference between the two groups on the total amount of money borrowed, both in time 0 and in time 1.

However, from the descriptions we noted that, after 12 months, women who have been successful have asked for larger amount of loans as opposed to women who have not been success.

Also the percentages of women with negative outcome, that have not remained active during the entire program of credit (inactive members) or who have left Grameen following problems in the process of extinction of the loan (left Grameen), is greater than women with positive outcomes. These findings support the hypothesis that women with negative outcomes have clearly met more obstacles during the loan program.

There were no significant differences between the two groups in relation to the loan user and the manager of it, in the sense that for both groups it appears to have been the husband. From a descriptive point of view the results show that in both groups of women, after 12 months, the percentage of wives who directly benefited from the loan increased, as did the percentage of spouses who shared the use of the loan. The percentage of husbands who benefited independently from the loan consequently decreased. This indicates that the outcome of the loan does not depend on the family member who uses it, and that regardless of success and failure, the percentage of women who agree to use the loan autonomously increased.

In addition, it is noted that the management of the loan is well distributed between the spouses in both successful families and in families who failed.

The percentage of loan management refers to the effective decision-making power that each spouse was able to exercise in order to monitor the outcome of the business. Similarly, there were no significant differences between the two groups with regard to the type of loan that is mostly invested in business. It detects a higher percentage of overlapping among women with negative outcomes (24%) and women with positive outcome (14.9%)

The balance changes in favor of a decrease in family decision-making power of the husband and increased decision-making power exercised jointly by both spouses. The presence of elements of conflict between the spouses is shown above in the analysis of family relationships (Network Chart). Women who have benefited from access to credit have started a process of mediation with their husbands, on the other hand, women who did not get benefits, initiated or exacerbated marital conflict.

This could be due to the fact that, through micro-credit, the beneficiaries acquire greater autonomy in economic and social terms, thus increasing their power within the decision-making process. This acquisition of autonomy, albeit modest, may result in the alteration of the previous family dynamics. Judging from the relational maps, there were significant changes in the relationship with their husbands, which sometimes manifested itself with a sentimental approach and sometimes with a departure and a worsening of the quality of relationships. In both instances this entailed major changes in family structures that could be the starting point for the questioning of a marital relationship based on a state of total subordination of women. From this point of view, microcredit does not disappoint in qualifying itself as a functional tool that triggers a process of change in the status of women within a socio-economic and cultural tradition in favor of men. Considering the vital importance of the husband's role in the mediation between the economic activity of their wife and the external market, it would seem reasonable to assume that women with negative results have failed to establish an alliance with their husband, one that ensures the development process of the family, probably due to a preexisting level of empowerment and greater access to credit.

CONCLUSION

The results indicate on average a positive impact in the microcredit program in both the personal and family life of the beneficiaries of the Grameen Bank.

We can therefore conclude that, scaling expectations on the impact of microcredit and the miraculous properties that has been covered in recent years, the program of the Grameen Bank proves to have a positive influence on the lives of poor households in developing countries. To take full advantage of the potential promised one does not need exceptional resources from the individuals involved, but rather favorable family circumstances are needed. It is also important to point out that the realization of a future follow-up could reverse the situation, especially in relation to women with negative outcomes. In this sense, the literature on microcredit suggests that, in some cases, women with greater empowerment, in light of the challenges put in place by cultural axioms, are characterized by a path of slower and gradual growth.

References

Ackerly, B. A. (1995). Testing the tools of development: Credit Programmes, loan involvement and women empowerment, *IDS Bulletin, Vol. 26 No.3*, pp. 56-68.

Ahmed, S.M., Chowdhury, M., & Bhuiya, A. (2001). Micro-credit and emotional well-being: experience of poor rural women from Matlab, Bangladesh. *World Development, 29(11),* pp. 1957-1966.

Armendariz de Aghion, B., & Murduch, J. (2000). Microfinance Beyond Group Lending. *Economics of Transition, 8(2),* pp. 401-420.

Brett, J. (2006). "We Sacrifice and Eat Less": The Structural Complexities of Microfinance Participation. *Human Organization, 65(1),* pp. 8-19.

Busza, J., & Porter, J. D. H. (2006). Effect of a structural intervention for the prevention of intimate-partner violence and HIV in rural South Africa: a cluster randomized trial. *Lancet, 368,* pp. 1973-1983.

CGAP (2003). Poverty Assessment Tool. *Technical Tools Series No. 5*, World Bank. http://www.cgap.org/sites/default/files/CGAP-Technical-Guide-Microfinance-Poverty-Assessment-Tool-Sep-2003.pdf

Costello, E.J. (1991). Married with children: predictors of mental and physical health in middle-aged women. *Psychiatry 1991, 54(3),* pp. 292-305.

Fernald, L., Hamad, R., Karlan, D., Ozer, E., & Zinman, J. (2008) Small Individual Loans and Mental Health: A Randomized Controlled Trial Among South African Adults. *BMC Public Health,* 8 (1), pp. 409.

Goetz, A. M., & SenGupta, R. (1996). Who Takes the Credit? Gender, Power, and Control over Loan Use in Rural Credit Programs in Bangladesh. *World Development, 24(1),* pp. 45-63.

Holvoet, N. (2005). The Impact of Microfinance on Decision-Making Agency: Evidence from South India. *Development and Change, 36(1),* pp. 75-102.

Kabeer, N. (2001). Conflicts over Credit: Re-Evaluating the Empowerment Potential of Loans to Women in Rural Bangladesh. *World Development, 29(1),* pp. 63-84.

Karlan, D. (2001). Microfinance impact assessments: the perils of using new members as a control group. *Journal of Microfinance, 3(2),* pp. 75-85.

Karlan, D., & Goldberg, N. (2007). The Impact of Microfinance: A Review of Methodological Issues. *Poverty Reduction and Economic Management (PREM),* World Bank, Nov 2000.

Kim, J. C., Watts, C. H. , Hargreaves, J. R., Ndhlovu, L. X. , Phetla, G., Morison, L. A., Busza, J., Porter, J. D. H., & Pronyk, P. M. (2007). Understanding the impact of a microfinance-based intervention on women's empowerment and the reduction of intimate partner violence in South Africa. *The American Journal of Public Health, 97(10),* pp. 1794-1802.

Koster, A., Bosma, H., Kempen, G. I., Penninx, B. W., Beekman, A. T., Deeg, D. J., & Van Eijk, J. T. (2006). Socioeconomic differences in incident depression in older adults: The role of psychosocial factors, physical health status, and behavioral factors. *Journal of Psychosomatic Research, 61(5),* pp. 619-627.

Littlefield, E., Morduch, J., & Hashemi, S. (2003). Is microfinance an effective strategy to reach the Millennium Development Goals? *CGAP Focus Note No. 24,* Washington, D.C.

Mayoux, L. (1998). Women's empowerment and micro-finance programmes: strategies for increasing impact. *Development in Practice, 8(2),* pp. 235-241.

Mohindra, K. S., & Haddad, S. (2005). Women's interlaced freedoms: A framework linking microcredit participation and health. *Journal of Human Development, 6,* pp. 353-374.

Mohindra, K., Haddad, S., & Narayana, D. (2008). Can microcredit help improve the health of poor women? Some findings from a cross-sectional study in Kerala, India. *International Society for Equity in Health, 10(7),* p. 2.

Muntaner, C., Eaton, W., Miech, R., & O'Campo, P. (2004). Socioeconomic Position and Major Mental Disorders. *Epidemiologic Reviews, 26,* pp. 53-62.

Nigeria: Case Study of Esan Women. *Journal of Asian and African Studies,42(6),* pp. 479-494.

Omorodion, F. I. (2007). Rural Women's Experiences of Micro-Credit Schemes in

Patel, V., & Kleinman, A. (2003). Poverty and common mental disorders in developing countries. *Bull WHO 81(8)*, pp. 609-615.

Prince, M., Patel, V., Saxena, S., Maj, M., Maselko, J., Phillips, M., & Rahman, A. (2007). No health without mental health. Lancet, 370(9590), pp. 859-77.

Schuler, S. R., Hashemi, S. M., Riley, A. P., & Akhter, A. (1996). Credit programs, patriarchy and men's violence against women in rural Bangladesh. *Social Science and Medicine, 43(12),* pp. 1729-1742.

Sharif, N. (2004). Microcredit programs and women's decision-making status: further evidence from Bangladesh. *Canadian Journal of Development Studies, 25(3),* pp. 465-480.

Simanowitz, A., & Walter, A. (2002). *Ensuring impact reaching the poorest while building financially self-sufficient institutions, and showing improvement in the lives of the poorest women and their families.* In S. Daley-Harris (Ed.) *Pathways Out of Poverty: Innovations in Microfinance for the Poorest Families.* Bloomfield, CT: Kumarian Press, Inc.

White, S. C. (1992). *Arguing with the Crocodile. Gender and Class in Bangladesh,* London: Zed Books.

In: The Other Side of the Coin
Editors: L. Brunori and M. Pines
ISBN: 978-1-62618-726-9

CONCLUSION

MICROCREDIT COMMUNITY AT STAKE: FROM IDEALIZATION TO DEMONIZATION TOWARDS TAKING RESPONSIBILITY

Microcredit has been seen, since its inception as one of the most revolutionary and challenging tool for economical growth based on social development in the last decades, and has been able to develop individuals and communities all over the world both economically, socially and psychologically.

Microcredit has been able to open people's heart to hope and, as a consequence, has been idealized and seen often as "the" resolution to all problems for poor people. Despair, in fact, tends to produce a need of hope that is comparable to a corresponding lack or fear not to have it. However, in spite of the fact that microcredit could not be the "resolutor" of all problems of the world, its philosophy and application have been able to mobilize more that 250 million people engaged in microcredit in different ways.

THE PROCESS OF CHANGE BETWEEN MESSIAH AND DEVIL

Like any innovative idea, it has been seen in an emotional area located in the social mental representation between Messiah and Devil: between hope and fear.

Hope for those who could have had the opportunity to change their status, and fear for those people (mostly Institutions) who could have had bad or uncontrolled consequences by the presence of this new idea and for those whose identity would have been affected by this innovation: for example Banks and the credit system. In this experience almost all economical and governmental agencies for credit are involved, often being unwilling to be responsible for poor people difficulties.

The proposal that MC offers is to change the status quo related to the possibility that each person in the world should have a chance, a credit; looking at credit as a human right.

Something totally different from the present situation as Yunus explains presenting Grameen Bank in public: "if you want to know how we operate, think of how banks operate and imagine that we do exactly the opposite [..] Banks give loans to rich people with collaterals, we give to poor people on trust, banks give money only to men in Bangladesh, we give money mostly to women" (Yunus, 2009)

So that it is obviously understandable the reaction that has developed against these proposals as in these actions there is a criticism, not always implicit, to the status quo and the Institutions involved.

It is common sense to say that present situation must be changed especially after the big economical crisis that the so called *developed world* has faced during the recent years. However the process that change has to go through, elicits, besides other aspects, a wide span of emotional reactions often at a very high level.

This is part of the situation when many attacks have been made towards different microcredit agencies, firstly against the founder of microcredit, the innovator: M. Yunus. The starting of this phenomenon is something also related to events concerned with political competition. In fact, political choices are also a main aspect involved in the process.

On these data, many emotional reactions have been activated by a kind of deception that microcredit was not seen anymore as "the solution" of economical problems in the world, produced the effect to see microcredit as the opposite.

Many more considerations could be offered about the changing process itself touching, besides the banks, some of the organizations that, by definition, exist in relation to the needs of the poor people that often are based on power management while taking care of those people. All organizations around the world whose activity is based on charity and that are facing, through microcredit application, a risk as being ineffective, and so requested to change their working programs including professional identities and relations amongst people involved.

We should consider those aspects related to the identity of operators, both in terms of professionalism and in terms of a narcissistic gain for charitable actions.

As for what concerns the "gender issue" related to microcredit that, as it is known, is mostly applied to women.

The revolutionary content of microcredit is intuitive as it is not only a means for economic education of women, nor a mere loan giving. What is most important is the recruitment of people engaged in this process to sign both with understanding and concretely a commitment to follow a set of rules that, in Grameen language are called "the 16 decisions".

The 16 decisions are a set of rules designed to prevent some cultural and social customs based mostly on women exploitation but not only so, that tend to maintain a so called vicious circle of poverty that often is generated, kept and even enhanced. As a consequence, again, it is understandable the social concern developed towards this process; another reaction to an important process of change!

MICROCREDIT IDENTITY

This is really what we could call a "hot point". As we said before, Microcredit from its inception has brought about great emotional reactions; I would say "a flood of hope".

Many different applications have been realized; so much so that a more precise definition of the microcredit Grameen model has been needed, just to avoid confusion. Of course differences in culture deserved such a differentiation in the application in different countries; however what has been lost sometimes in this adaptation has been the meaning of the process and the *raison d'être* of it.

In Nusa Dua, Bali in 2008, during the Microcredit Summit, the point was made especially in relation to the profit making structure and to the profit maximizing philosophy of microcredit enterprises.

The occasion derived from an event that happened in Mexico where *"Compartamos"*, a microcredit Agency, appeared to make profit on poor people shoulders without any recognition to them.

Vice versa, Grameen Bank is owned mostly by its beneficiaries with only a small participation by the State; in other words it is shaped in a way that Yunus calls Social Business.

The definition of "social business" was clarified in that occasion: *no loss, no dividend* as a chosen structure to develop and contain such a delicate process.

This is only one of the "*identifiable*" aspects of microcredit. There are other delicate parts of the whole microcredit process that have to do with the procedures related to the relational system; one of these is related to the devices through which money is being given; inside which relational system occurs the exchange and the agreement with the beneficiaries and the surrounding community.

Great deal of attention is paid in the Grameen model to the educational side and to the relational one; this is one of the reasons for the creation of groups and for the reinforcement of beneficial and significant social links.

As already said it's a device that, while giving value to the group as a whole, is able to value, in the mean time, its members as individuals in a relational win-win dynamic.

The training that is given to Grameen borrowers aims at helping these persons to understand both rules and possibilities in the entrepreneurial activity and to "evaluate" their "capabilities" through experience.

This is of course something that is strongly needed if the intention is to help persons that deserve to be supported in this process of growth and change of an identity based on totally different cultural assumptions.

Poor people, as it is epidemiologically evident all over the world, either try to overcome their status through disobedience to rules that appear not to be friendly with them and keep them out of the social community in those conditions, or let passivity and depression to take away their vital energy.

What is intended to do with microcredit is to re-start from those energies transforming the vicious circle into a virtuous one for the individuals and the Community.

From this perspective, so, as we have seen in various chapters of this volume, the process has to be seen to be composed of two aspects equally important and inter-related: one *tangibile*, made of concrete and visible results and one *intangibile*, made of relationships and mental self representations and of the surrounding world modified by this experience and their new way of coping with.

Both achievements are important and we could even say that the money can be seen as a pretext for what some consider being fuel and *raison d'être* of the whole: the transformation of a sense of "*shame to exist*" into a sense of "*pride to be able to*".

The group, in all this process, is the relational tool to realize and contain the whole changing process that implies, as it is evident, several aspects. A circular dialogue, starting from individuals, through families, communities and society, that, at the end, gives benefits to the individuals with whom the process started.

What is evident is that we are talking of a "*bottom up*" process and you can immediately guess its political and educational value and consequences.

Scopes and intentions may be clear. What is not always so clear is the understanding of the consequences of the methodologies applied, mostly for what concerns the relational aspects connected to "*good enough*" professionalism in the field.

Besides that, if group is the basic tool, high knowledge in group processes and its consequences on individuals should be given to those who operate in the field.

Microcredit identity should be clarified as well in terms of the agreements developed between borrowers and practitioners, and all related methodologies which make a real difference in the definition of the instrument and the consequences on the people. So that, in order to summarize, we should imagine microcredit identity delineated between all actors of the whole scenario, facing the relational aspects of it with the will to take common responsibility for the whole Microcredit Community:

- between borrowers and practitioners
- between borrowers themselves
- between agencies
- between agencies and political government
- between agencies and other NGO or similar.

Towards Responsibility for the Definition of Boundaries and Relations

All that has been said till now opens the need to face some problems in a coherent and responsible way, and to find some common and shared solutions. A need for a common and shared responsibility is at stake. A need to understand that an ethical attitude in this matter is not an option of good will, but a matter of "*professional technicalities*". All this is under discussion and requires a specific attention and sets of responsible commonly shared actions.

In this discussion what emerges, amongst others, is a need for understanding the outcome in a congruent and comprehensive way that gives reason to all aspects of the whole process.

A reflective function should be developed to allow all entities to be aware of right or distorted and even abusive ways in which microcredit could be applied both intentionally by lack of attention paid to the relational aspects of it or by mistake; what always can occur in human actions.

We do not think that you should doubt Microcredit's definition as a tool, thought imagined and applied to overcome poverty. The poor are the recipients and for them it should be designed and applied but in a way that gives back results also to those who take the responsibility to become entrepreneurs in the microcredit area in a way that is a win-win solution for both.

What is good or bad should be object of study and reflection by experts in the different disciplinary areas by which microcredit is composed and from the different institutional and organizational components that play a significant role.

The outcome of the whole again should be the proof that the aim is reached.

Cost-benefit evaluation is a practice that has been adopted in medical research on efficacy and efficiency in the frame of *Managed Care System*. This is something that should be applied systematically for evaluating the outcome, comparing different applications looking for the best practices having in mind the protection of a tool that, relationally speaking, is based on trust: strength and weakness of it at the same time.

Time has arrived to design an "organizational worldwide protection system" able to take the responsibility for the whole process.

This idea has led Microcredit Summit, the most important worldwide organization to generate an instrument; the Seal of Excellence aiming at clarifying some of the aspects that we are discussing here.

Actors and representatives are involved in it, some independent experts included, to develop a system watching for the possible "*best quality*" applied in the microcredit action.

This initiative means an assumption of responsibility, overcoming infinite discussion on what is "the best way" or "the worst", without paying attention to all variables and taking into account all aspects and players in the field.

We could take this action as an opportunity to develop a reasonable and needed reflective function to keep and ameliorate the whole service through the assumption of responsibility of the monitoring process defined and acquired, as a common need focused on a continuing learning process.

Responsibility as we have already said is the key word from several points of view.

The struggles that are going on amongst MFI accepted as an expression of a free market philosophy are highly pernicious for our work and mostly for poor people for evident many reasons: the most important one is the risk to destroy trust and hope that are both the fuel and the *raison d'être* of the whole story.

The philosophy behind microcredit is not that of the Darwinian struggle for survival in the jungle, where the stronger wins and the others loose; it is more that of a shared responsibility for something common that is the survival of humanity as such and in the quality of relations between the persons.

Microcredit can be seen as well as common goods, something that, starting from Yunus idea, expanded all over the world as an expression of economical need but, at the same time, an expression of a need for survival for all human beings. Microcredit experience can offer an opportunity to better distribute the resources in the world that now are divided in a way where 20% of world wide population owns the 80%. We cannot call this situation economic in the sense of "*oikòs nomos*" (X) because the *rules of the family home* are totally disregarded as such. The world family of human beings needs to recognize the need for mirroring between humans and all human resonance that can be developed through coherent conditions and political actions.

Another important aspect is the need for professional training for operators applied in different ways in the microcredit field. Education has to be both Basic and Continuing to guarantee a continuing process of learning and must regard legal and banking technicalities, socio-economical and anthropological knowledge, psychological for what concerns the relational aspects. Some agreements on a basic syllabus could be a good initiative for the creation of a minimum standard as it happens internationally for other disciplines and professions.

We repeat here how important it would be to be able to reach an agreement between Microcredit agencies available to develop a planning based on values of effectiveness and efficiency, planning a systematic monitoring of the experiences also through compared studies aiming at "protecting" the good quality of a project seen and felt as common good for all parties involved and of the whole Microcredit Community that could appear, in doing so, able to take the responsibility to overcome the situation where MC is neither the Messiah nor the Devil but something run by human beings at risk to mistake like all human being actions, made by human beings to help other human beings to reach a more human life that all deserve.

Index

A

B

C

D

E

F

G

H

I

J

K

L

M

N

O

P

Q

R

S

T

U